THE CHURCH
WEDDING
HANDBOOK

The Reverend Giles Legood is a
Church of England priest who is
working as a university chaplain in the
Diocese of London. In his present post
and previously in parish ministry he
has helped many couples prepare for
their wedding day. He is editor of
Chaplaincy – the Church's Sector Ministries
and *Veterinary Ethics – an Introduction*.

Professor Ian Markham is the
Foundation Dean and Professor of
Theology and Public Life at Liverpool
Hope University College. He has taught
theology to university students,
ordination candidates, church groups
and others for many years. His previous
books include *Plurality and Christian
Ethics* and *Truth and the Reality of God*.

The authors met as students at King's
College London and have previously
produced *The Godparents' Handbook*
together. Giles Legood and Ian Markham
are both married.

Also by the same authors

The Godparents' Handbook, 1997, SPCK

THE CHURCH WEDDING HANDBOOK

GILES LEGOOD
and
IAN MARKHAM

First published in Great Britain in 2000 by
Society for Promoting Christian Knowledge
Holy Trinity Church
Marylebone Road
London NW1 4DU

Bible quotations are from the *New Revised Standard Version
of the Bible* © 1989 by the Division of Christian Education
of the National Council of the Churches of Christ in the USA.

British Library Cataloguing-in-Publication Data

A catalogue record for this book is available from
the British Library

ISBN 0-281-05269-7

Typeset by Pioneer Associates, Perthshire
Printed in Great Britain by
Omnia Books Ltd, Bishopbriggs, Glasgow

To our parents-in-law

Sheila and Malcolm
Kathleen and John

with love

Contents

Introduction

The Christian Churches touch the lives of countless millions of people in many different ways. Many who find themselves on the edge of the Christian community for much of the time still want to engage with the Church at important moments in their lives – at birth, marriage or death (the so-called moments of being 'hatched, matched and despatched'). Such contacts should be welcomed and affirmed by the Churches.

When a couple discover love, and in the fullness of time want to celebrate this love with others and make a public declaration of living together in love for all time, they often feel that the occasion needs to be celebrated in a church. Like them we believe that the discovery of love is indeed one which ought to be celebrated in church, because love is the very reason for our being, and that God to whom the Churches bear witness is the source of life and love. In writing this book, therefore, we want to encourage couples to use their wedding preparations as an opportunity to reflect on the big questions of life while also offering them help with the intensely practical and necessary tasks surrounding any wedding.

When a baby arrives, parents often want the child baptized and, as part of this, godparents appointed to be involved in the child's upbringing. In *The Godparents' Handbook* we attempted to encourage those who feel this way and we also wanted to encourage the future godparents who found themselves cast in this new role to enjoy the honour and privilege, to use the opportunity to forge a distinctive relationship with the child and to reflect seriously on the Christian context of the baptism service and the promises it contains.

All books concerned with pastoral and practical theology are, or should be, results of an enterprise shared with others. In our cases we want to thank the institutions in which we work and significant people in them. Professor Simon Lee of Liverpool Hope and the Reverend Stephen Williams, Senior University Chaplain in the Diocese of London, are model colleagues in offering friendship, support and encouragement. We are pleased to be able to take this opportunity to acknowledge what we have learnt from them. To the many friends, both single or married, straight or gay, whose company we have enjoyed and who have helped shape the attitudes that pervade the book we owe grateful thanks. We are grateful also to Simon Kingston of SPCK for supporting us in this book and in *The Godparents' Handbook*, both of which endeavour to connect with those on the edges of the life of the Church. Being concerned as we are with higher education, we wish to thank those young people with whom we work who have informed our knowledge and understanding of the nature of relationships, love and marriage. The love we receive in our own respective home lives also inspires and delights us. Immeasurable thanks are due therefore to Lesley and Luke Markham and to Melanie Phillips.

Finally, we would like to dedicate this book to our parents-in-law. A wedding emphasizes and celebrates the importance of love between a couple, but also makes a significant connection between families. For the love, kindness and support which we have found in the families we have joined through marriage, we are enormously grateful.

CHAPTER ONE

Looking at Ourselves

You are in love and you are thinking about getting married. This is the reason, presumably, why you find yourself holding a book written by a priest and a professor of theology about marriage. Being in love is, of course, the best reason for getting married, and on one level, it all ought to be so simple. Yet perhaps you are already discovering that once the matter of marriage has been raised, suddenly it all becomes rather complicated.

Complexities arise for several reasons. Two individuals who find themselves in love is one thing, although even here things can sometimes get complicated. However, two people who decide that they want recognition by families, friends and society in the act of holy matrimony is quite another thing. Deciding to get married is definitely a decision to move beyond the private and personal relationship in such a way that others are bound to be affected. Mum and Dad have a new member of their family; the family Christmas will include your partner. Brothers and sisters will lose the 'exclusive' nature of your relationship and will have to share you with someone else. Friends have to cope with the eccentricities and preoccupations of the person you have decided to marry.

The decision to get married will provoke a whole range of conflicting feelings that are both inevitable and sometimes difficult. People often moan about the way 'the wedding' gets taken over, but this is simply the inevitable result of people adjusting to what is about to take place. Mum adjusting to her 'little boy' becoming a man; Dad adjusting to a rival for his daughter's affections; and siblings and friends adjusting to the changing dynamics as your partner becomes part of the furniture of their lives. There is no way these complexities can be avoided. Relationships, even when you are 12 and simply dating that spotty teenager down the road, involve and affect others. Once you get older and rightly want others to recognize the love you have discovered, then the involvement of others becomes much more marked. It was ever thus.

However, life in the twenty-first century is a little more complicated. There was a time when the majority of people getting married were doing so for the first time: now that is less true. Many people are living together before they decide to get married. Those coming to marriage while having to cope with the hurt and disappointment of a previously failed marriage or those who have seen partners die and are now hoping for a fresh start will find the whole process even more complicated. Whether you are leaving home, marrying after many years of a single life, cohabiting happily with your partner, coping with the breakdown of an early marriage, or coping with

5

losing an earlier partner, there are different issues involved. We are now going to look at those issues. We suggest you simply read the section appropriate for you and then press on with Chapter 2.

Leaving home

This is how we imagine it will be for all of us when we are young. We all imagine that as we grow up we will meet someone, fall in love, leave home and get married. We even pencil in a date. We will finish school, get a job, work for a few years, perhaps travel, perhaps go to university, and then we will get married. We will be in our twenties; we might even pencil into our life-plan a couple of children before we reach 30. For some people this is how it happens. School and university years are good opportunities to meet people. We are surrounded by lots of people our age, there is plenty of choice, and it is relatively easy for someone to become a 'significant other'. If we are lucky, we might have several years to accustomize our families to our significant other; they almost expect the wedding and just wait for the announcement.

For all its delightful predictability there are still certain pressures. The most significant is the accusation that 'you are simply too young'. Age for the 'leaving home' marriage is one of the trickiest issues. It is true that marriage does require considerable commitment and therefore maturity. It is preferable that one has developed the necessary emotional maturity to cope with the demands of marriage. Although legally you can be married at 16, the advice of those who suggest that one should wait a while is good. Sixteen is the point at which life suddenly speeds up. This is well documented. When you move from age four to age five, everything seems to drag: Christmas is still an age away and that special treat seems to involve an eternity of waiting. The reason for this is that you are living a fifth of your entire life. When you move from 36 to 37, Christmas seems to be followed seconds later by another Christmas. The routines of life are rapid and dramatic. At 16 you are in the period of the change. To be 18 or 19 might still seem a long wait, but in actual fact it comes much quicker than you expect.

There are two reasons why some people contemplate getting married at 16. First, they are committed Christians who think that marriage is the setting for sex. Second, the partner is a great deal older than 16 and especially eager to get married sooner rather than later.

Sex will show up again later in the book. Suffice it to say at this stage, there is something good, healthy and fun about enjoying the platonic world of friendship which stops well short of sex. Sex is extremely significant but it can complicate the world considerably. At 16, being willing to wait for that is extremely wise.

Age, then, is often the first issue for the young 'leaving home' type. The second – pressure from an older partner to get married younger – should be simply resisted. Resorting to a young marriage is sometimes indicative of various insecurities. So, for example, where there is a lack of love in one's life, one might desperately seek the reassurance that marriage can bring. This is where waiting can help. Self-knowledge about one's insecurities (and we all have them) comes with age. Knowledge of your partner's problems comes with a deepening and developing relationship. Allow the relationship to grow prior to getting married. In this way the marriage is more likely to succeed.

If your partner has been part of your life for several years and the expectation of a marriage announcement is high, then adjustment can be easy for your relatives and friends. If it comes as a semi-shock, then it can be tricky. For this group, the rule is simple: show understanding. You would not want people to take your decision lightly or to be indifferent to it. The questions, the doubts and the earnest conversations all reflect love and care. They should be tolerated and answered directly.

Naturally doubts from others can become excessive. Where there is prejudice of a racial or religious nature, then one must politely refuse to respond to the critical comment. Where the reassurance fails to reassure, you are entitled to fall back on your legal entitlement to make a decision and live with the consequences. Always try to keep family and friends on board (so avoid the blazing row and slamming doors scenario), but if you are sure then you must be free to exercise your decision.

Once the decision has been made and family and friends informed, those who are leaving home to get married will find the rest of the process relatively straightforward. Clergy know and understand this group of people. Family and friends will enjoy the occasion. You are now ready to press on with Chapter 2.

Single, then 'Surprise!'

The fashion in many ways is to wait for marriage. Commitment is something we fear. School passes, university may come and go, and we embark on the world of work. 'Young, free and single' is the slogan; we are called 'an eligible bachelor' or a 'single girl'. We are not tied down and we can still have fun.

However, the shock for some is the way in which the world of work proves so inhospitable. From thousands (literally in some places) of eligible people at university, we suddenly find ourselves in an office with six other people, five of whom are married and the one single person is heavily into trainspotting. Singleness, which was a matter of delight and pride, suddenly can become a source of anxiety and fear. Dating agencies and singles bars are ways to transcend the lack of options in the modern office. Then, despite such methods, as if by chance you suddenly meet someone who is the 'right person' and marriage becomes an option. It is natural for many in these situations to marry quite quickly. The 'courtship' for a 35-year-old can be very quick – sometimes less than a year.

Normally it is the speed that can create the complications. Single people are often very precious friends.

9

If you want to 'count' or 'rely' on a friend, it is much easier if they are single. Marriage brings a set of commitments that makes the 'let's hit the town' suggestion tricky. The task in this situation is to prepare your friends with care. You may have to cope with jealously and disappointment and, if possible, the best thing to do is to be generous in allowing your friends to adjust.

The other feature of the 'single then surprise' type is that expectations of love might be significantly reduced. Romantic love is a delicious delight of life, but it is not for everyone. It is possible that this type is in the first instance searching for a friend or a companion and therefore skips the 'romantic love' phase. A love built on friendship emerges – a love which recognizes faults and makes allowances. Although others will be shocked by the seeming lack of passion, in actual fact this can be a very good foundation for marriage.

Living with a partner and then marriage

One of the most common patterns in the lives of people preparing to get married is that of having lived with their partner for a year or more and then deciding that they would like to get married. There is a widespread feeling that 'cohabitation' is sensible as it means that prior to making those dramatic promises you are able to check that you can live with your partner.

It is true that many cohabiting couples demonstrate

all the commitment of a marriage. There can be fidelity, love and mutual understanding. However, some Christians have found cohabitation a problem. First, it involves 'sex outside marriage', which as we shall see later is considered wrong. The home for sexual activity is marriage; this is the environment where the promises have been made that protect the ultimate significance of the sexual act. Second, there is a belief that cohabitation is more likely to lead to divorce. Indeed there is some statistical evidence for this claim. But the truth is that those who are willing to question tradition by cohabiting are also those willing to question the convention of staying in an unhappy marriage when things go wrong. In other words, it is a personality difference rather than cohabitation leading to more divorces.

However, for these two reasons, there can be problems when a cohabiting couple approaches a priest or minister asking for marriage. The traditional solution was a gentle deception: one person would put down their parent's address. However, it is such a commonplace these days, this deception is needed less and less.

There are two main reasons why cohabitation can become marriage. The first is that cohabitation marked the period of 'engagement' and the plan always was to marry and cohabitation is a form of experimentation in living together. The second is that the couple has decided they want children. It is this latter reason which can cause problems. The decision to abandon contraception and try for a child is an important one.

However, there is a significant possibility that the couple will have problems conceiving. Although 80 per cent of couples conceive in two years, that still leaves a puzzled, upset and disturbed 20 per cent. A marriage for children when the children do not come can put the marriage at risk. It is important that this issue is discussed prior to marriage. The decision to commit to each other in marriage has to be justified in its own right.

Coping with the breakdown of an earlier marriage

No family is untouched by the sadness of divorce. Every divorce is sad even if the couple separate amicably. It is not our task in this book to reflect on why people get divorced. There are numerous reasons; some people do just make a mistake. They find themselves married to entirely unsuitable partners. Women especially may suddenly decide that the 'patriarchal' partner is someone that they are not going to tolerate any longer, while others again find themselves 'in love' outside the marriage.

The biggest problem here is coping with the baggage and sometimes the damage caused by the earlier marriage, and often professional advice may be needed. It is important not to be afraid to confront the problems that created the difficulties. From a Christian point of view, it is important to stress that everything in the past can be forgiven. At the heart of the Christian story is the conviction that God has taken the confusion and mess of being human onto the cross and transformed it into the resurrection. Christians believe that God is able to take all our messes and muddles and transform them by grace.

Things can become complicated when those who are divorced and want to remarry wish to do so in a church. As we shall see later, Roman Catholic theology teaches that divorce is technically impossible. Once God has united two souls in the sacrament of marriage then no human can separate them: the only way out is through the technical provision of annulment (there wasn't a marriage in the first place). This can cause considerable pain. Strictly if one divorces and then remarries, one is in a state of sin which makes it impossible for you to take the Holy Mass. The Church of England is moving to a formal position where the 'innocent' party may remarry (although as we shall see, individual clergy may perform a marriage ceremony for anyone who is legally entitled to marry – including, of course, divorcees). This official position is difficult because it does require an examination of the 'causes' of a marriage breakdown. Given that knowledge of what exactly is happening in a marriage is available only to those involved, this can be difficult. Both the Roman Catholic Church and the Church of England offer a 'blessing' of the civil ceremony, where a couple get married in a registry office and then go to church for a service of blessing.

The Free Churches (Methodist, Baptists and United

Reformed) are much more flexible. They tend to consider the merits of each case. For Baptists, the stress tends to be on active participation in the Christian community, often over several years, which might enable them to 'marry' you. The United Reformed Church is less concerned with this requirement. If you find yourself in this position, the only way forward is to visit the various Christian clergy and discuss the details of your position. You will find that the practice can vary considerably, even from parish to parish.

The fact that you are interested in Church recognition is good. At its best the Church is a community of forgiveness, love and understanding. It is possible to witness to the demands and delights of a traditional marriage, while not turning it into a weapon to beat those who for whatever reason cannot live up to the expectations. Many ministers want to affirm and celebrate your discovery. The past can and should be forgiven.

Lost and found

The final group involves those who have already been married but tragically have lost their partner through death. In the single state once again they find someone else to whom they would like to get married.

It is very easy for a person to become accustomed to 'being married' and when the status changes, the need to remarry may become overwhelming. There is nothing wrong with this feeling nor is there anything wrong with the efforts made to find another marriage partner. The only possible danger is that the haste does not lead to an appropriate match. It remains important that any existing network of relationships survives the new marriage. Children are involved and need to be introduced early on to anyone being considered. Both partners must respect and come to terms with the past; it is tragic when a new partner insists on the destruction of all photographs of the past. A former marriage can and should be celebrated, even as one embarks on a new one. In fact, problems in this area are relatively rare, and age and maturity almost certainly help. Most Christian communities and many friends and families are often ready to assist as the new marriage emerges.

Self-knowledge and marriage

As you embark on this journey towards marriage, whichever of the positions described above you come from, the primary need is to be self-aware. Marriage requires a certain combination of maturity and self-knowledge. It is important to acknowledge the complexities in your situation and to confront the adjustments that others will have to make because of your decision to marry. We conclude this chapter with a few questions you might like to think about.

1 At what point did I realize I wanted to get married?
2 Are there any complications in my past that I need to recognize and confront?
3 Are there others in the present situation whom I

need to handle with particular sensitivity as they come to terms with the news of my forthcoming marriage?

4 Am I being honest with both my future partner and myself?

CHAPTER TWO

Deciding to Get Married

Marriage is definitely under attack. Although many millions of people continue to decide for marriage (some on their second or third time around), the whole idea of fidelity and monogamy is not popular. If you study the numerous magazines that are preoccupied with sexual activity on our news-stands, you will find that a very simple, anti-marriage ethic is being advocated. The ethic starts from the correct and true premise that sex is delightful. Sex is one of life's great experiences but, as with most great experiences – so the argument develops – the greater the quantity and variety the better. To confine sexual activity to one person is a needless limitation.

At this point an analogy might be offered. When they are in their mid- to late teenage years, many people move away from drinking cider and discover the delights of beer and wine. Many start by drinking sugary, sweet wines. Now it would be tragic to insist that 'monogamy' required complete fidelity to the wine which is initially tried – Lambrusco in many cases. Surely it is wiser to move on and try different wines and grapes, and discover the infinite variety of wines there are to be enjoyed, perhaps a claret, a Sémillon or a Californian Chardonnay.

At this point, some Christians might be horrified. It sounds like there are no rules at all. That is not true. The Letters pages in the magazines on the news-stands set out the rules with some care. First, all sexuality must involve informed consent. Any coercion at all is strictly forbidden. Naturally child abuse, rape and bestiality are completely wrong. But less obviously, it is also wrong for an older lad to promise the world to a younger girl just to get her into bed. There is an expectation that sexual activity should be confined to consenting adults. There is a requirement for people to take 'responsibility' for their sexual activity and so it is important to use contraception. But providing these rules are met, sex with a variety of partners (preferably one after another, not concurrently) is acceptable.

Further arguments are offered in support of this position. To decide at the age of 20 to promise oneself to one person is madness. You might change or the other person might change. You might find someone else or the other person might find someone else. In short, a promise of monogamy is very unwise. The more sophisticated suggest that the Church's ambiguous attitude has confined sex for too long to marriage. Many friendships with both genders are 'sexual' and recognition of this is long overdue. Allowing sexual expression to spill out rather more often among friends would be healthy and good.

Two other arguments against marriage are worth noting. Both have their roots within the ideology of communism. It was Engels who complained that the roots of marriage are in capitalist anxieties concerning property. The historic problem for a man was simple: how can I make sure that I pass on my property to a blood relative? It is always obvious who the mother of a child is, but it is less obvious who was involved nine months beforehand. To guarantee the property line, marriage was invented, Engels argued. The prison of the family guarantees the succession of property, from father to son. It also provides a cheap form of labour which can be exploited. Mothers are domestic slaves who keep a clean house, provide meals and offer a child-rearing service.

It was this latter point that led to the feminist critique of the traditional marriage and family. Marriages are often very patriarchal institutions (i.e. ruled by and in the interests of men). The man is in control: he is, to use biblical terminology, the head of the household. Marriage serves male needs: the woman is left at home to serve the male. The place of the woman is in the bed (providing sexual satisfaction for the male) and the kitchen (providing meals), with permission to clean the rest of the house en route between these two rooms.

The result of all these arguments taken together is that marriage is now very definitely out of fashion, or at least to be more accurate, many participate in marriages but few are persuaded of its virtues. The modern attitude to sex has come about for one major reason. Contraception makes it possible for two people to have sex without having children. It creates the option of promiscuity; and we now live in a culture where many people are promiscuous.

So the challenge 'why marry?' needs to be thought through with some care. Let us now examine the counter case. We start by attacking the anti-marriage argument. There are two problems with it: first, we need to be able to cope with the unpredictability of the future; second, marriage is the best way to enjoy both sexual quantity and quality. We will start by examining these two problems first.

Coping with the future

The argument against marriage is the argument of the young. It is no coincidence that the ethic outlined is promulgated most strongly in the magazines that target the 20- to 35-year-old age range. *Cosmopolitan* and *Men's Health* are two such magazines. The argument assumes it is most readily acceptable to a person who is relatively young and has plenty of choices. It is an ethic only really available to the young, relatively good-looking, relatively affluent and relatively healthy. It targets individuals who treat sex and relationships in the same way as wine; that is to say people who, in the end, use others for their own satisfaction.

However, we all know that living is precarious. The young grow old; the good-looking become wrinkly; the affluent go through difficult times; and the healthy become sick. Problems touch all human lives and we need institutions that provide defences against such problems.

Families are the most important fortress against the precarious nature of life. Plenty of adults suddenly discover the need for parents and siblings as problems emerge. Parents, brothers and sisters are always there to support, help, provide a home and pay off a credit card debt! The family is built on a marriage. Ideally the marriage should not simply provide you with a fortress against the inevitable difficulties of life, but can become a haven for others. Living as an isolated individual is the dream of some, but the reality is that we all need support. Marriage is intended to provide that.

Quantity and quality

Our opponent of marriage made much of the mistake of monogamy. It was argued that as with all good experiences you should go for quantity (many different partners) and the quality (tasting the variety). So we arrive at a vision of moving from one sexual encounter to another and enjoying the quantity and quality of the experiences.

However, for many who are 'young, free and single', the number of encounters is often few and the quality can be poor. First, on the quantity argument: there is little question that most people who are married have many more sexual encounters than single people do. It is the very fact that one is with one person, where there is an understanding that there is a sharing of physical intimacy as a part of the relationship, which almost guarantees more sexual encounters. Granted these are all with the same person, but the fact is that generally speaking married people have more sex than single people.

On the quality front, it is also clear that most good marriages produce better sex. Sex is difficult. Drunk fumbling after a night out at a club is unlikely to produce quality sex. To achieve sexual contentment requires a knowledge of your partner's needs and to attain such knowledge takes considerable time. Sex emerging from a committed relationship should be better sex. Most people look better with clothes on than off and so we need a trusting relationship in which we remove our clothes! This is the reason why, apart from one-night stands, most people involved in sexual relationships do become a couple. For a period, sometimes rather brief, the relationship becomes similar to a poor marriage. There will be some sort of commitment; there will be a mutual giving of one to the other; and there will a limited set of expectations (i.e. that they are 'there' for each other).

The fact is that the best sex involves at least a partial 'marriage'. The advantage of the real thing is that one locates the sex in real commitment to each other. It is at this point we turn to the argument from love.

The nature of love

It might seem mad to make a decision to love someone regardless of what happens but this is the nature of love. Let us consider the decision to have a child. The moment you embark on that journey you are making an open-ended decision. The birth of your child is the creation of a life that will always be in relationship with you. As the child emerges blinking and crying in the world, so a relationship begins which will exasperate and delight in almost equal measure. Although some parents do try to walk away from the relationship, in fact they cannot. Even an absentee father is still the actual, biological father of the child. Fortunately, however, most parents know that the relationship is simply a given that will have to endure the child's stupidity, unkindness, anger, disappointment and hurt as well as take delight in the good. Of course, the rewards are infinitely precious. Parents are the pillars which can make a child's life meaningful. The child learns to love through receiving good parenting and in turn lavishes much love upon the parents. The joy and happiness which children receive and give cannot be measured.

Historically the reason for monogamy and fidelity in marriage is that they provide the only context in which children can be brought up. The commitment which child-rearing requires – one which is open-ended and total – needs to be matched by a mutual commitment between the parents. The loving environment the child needs is often best served by a comparable love between the parents.

Married love, then, transcends the simply romantic. Romantic love occurs in that moment when you have strong and often overwhelming feelings for the other, when you are totally preoccupied with the other. It is a great feeling and many marriages have it in moments and phases, but the rock of the marriage is not necessarily this fabulous feeling, but the simple commitment to be with the other come what may.

Decision displaces the feeling. In the same way that a child is always one's child, so too the partner becomes quite simply always one's partner.

Marriage and exploitation

On one matter, however, we must give our opponent of marriage some credit. If a marriage is exploitative, then that is wrong. Of course, if there is love at the heart of a marriage then a marriage should not be exploitative. However, even today, there are people entering marriages with very traditional expectations of the relationship. This can be a source of considerable unhappiness. The fortress against the problems of life can also become a fortress where almost anything takes place. When people close the front door of a home, few others know for certain how people are behaving within that home. Sadly this is why abuse (verbal or physical and most often against children and women) can take place. It seems the ultimate act of humiliation to be required to admit that the place where one should be most secure is, in fact, a place of unspeakable cruelty and hurt. Less traumatic is the tendency for a couple just to lapse into different roles. The male role is to sit and command the remote control on the television, to put his feet up and to disappear periodically to the pub for a drink with his mates. The female role is to care for the children, clear up the house, provide meals, do all the washing, do all the ironing, and keep everything in order. Let us be quite clear: there is no reason for these roles.

Women are not better cooks; males are not unable to wash up and clear up. The male sex organ does not get in the way of the iron; there is no reason why a bloke cannot clean a lavatory.

One clear reason for marriage breakdown is that women are largely persuaded that these traditional roles have to go. Some men, sadly, have not realized this fact. They expect the wife to behave in the same way as their mother (it is odd how many patriarchal homes also extend the service provided to the husband to include the sons). The result is that the woman finally decides that she has had enough and the marriage breaks down.

Feminism is now a permanent feature of modern Western life and marriage must adapt to accommodate its essential moral insight. This insight is that men and women are equal. Therefore, in marital terms, a marriage is a partnership of equals and there must be a fair balance of duties and responsibilities within the home. The wife in a marriage is not a domestic servant to the husband. We believe that traditional patriarchal marriages will not survive. If the male partner cannot cope with the thought of his wife earning more than him, then he should not marry or should rethink his perspective. If the man is expecting a domestic servant and thinks this is right and proper, then he should be prepared for divorce. The 'slave woman' might, under the glare of romantic love, provide the service he expects and demands for a few years, but the wife may come to see things in a different light and hold the man responsible for his exploitation.

So why marry?

The best argument for marriage is the nature of love. One marries because one appreciates that the family is a unit dedicated to 'open-ended' love. As we will see later, the married family unit is a setting in which children can thrive. In the same way that a commitment to a child is open-ended, so it is with the commitment in marriage.

However, the reasons for marriage do need discussion. As you prepare for your marriage you need to discuss the roles each of you will be adopting, or already have adopted. Any patriarchal assumptions need to be challenged. It is essential that both partners enter a marriage committed to equality and mutual respect. We therefore conclude this chapter with a few questions for you to think about.

1 What is the point of getting married?
2 Can I handle fidelity and monogamy?
3 Why is it important that sex and love are woven together?
4 Is the Church right to teach that a loving, stable environment is the best environment for children to grow up in?
5 What roles should men and women play in marriage?

CHAPTER THREE

Christianity and Marriage

Having defended marriage in general in the last chapter, we now turn to consider the location and style of wedding celebrations. It will not surprise you to know that the authors of this book are strong advocates of church weddings. However, it is worth pausing and considering their main alternative.

We have the religious Reformation of the sixteenth century to thank for the option of a purely civil marriage ceremony. The German theologian and reformer Martin Luther and others all insisted that first and foremost a marriage is a civil ceremony, which must be recognized by society. Therefore, they argued, one of the most important parts of the ceremony is the participation of the witnesses from the community who confirm that the two people did exchange vows and are now married and therefore ready to play their full role in society in a new way. Today in Britain it is possible to have a civil ceremony in a variety of locations, although most opt for the traditional registry office. Armed with a box of tissues to distribute to tearful relatives and friends (hopefully tears of joy!), a civil registrar will perform the ceremony efficiently and effectively.

One of the positive attractions for some is that such weddings are less lavish. There are those who do not want the enormous build-up, the expenditure of thousands of pounds and the fuss. Some would rather take a day off work, pop down to the registry office and have a nice meal with a small group of family and close friends in the evening. This is no less a wedding, nor is it any less a marriage. The promises are still made and vows exchanged, the expectations are still there and there is no reason why it cannot be just as happy and committed as any other marriage.

Nevertheless as Christians, we would like to commend the church wedding option. This is not simply because churches provide a better location for the pictures, although often that is true, but because of the symbolism of marriage. The Christian Church, however, would want to go further and say that in discovering love one is discovering the purposes of being and that in making connections with a person at such a deep level, one is becoming fully human. This is the testimony of a church building. It has stood, in some cases for hundreds of years, as a testimony to God who is the source of life and love, and in this way it provides the perfect location for a wedding.

Christianity, of course, provides details about the reason why weddings capture these lives of love. Christians believe that we are not simply complex bundles of atoms, which emerged within a pointless universe and which face extinction when they die. Instead at the heart of the universe is goodness and love that enables everything that is to be. It is in the nature of love to be in relationship: you cannot love in a relationship of one. Christians therefore talk of God as a 'Trinity' (three persons, Father, Son and Holy Spirit, yet one God, all in relation). It is in the nature of love that one desires to create further loving possibilities (it is one of the reasons why so many married couples end up having children). Love creates. Christians need have no quarrel with the details of the scientific narrative which holds that 15 billion years ago a quantum fluctuation caused the universe to expand, that the factors that generated life coincided on planet earth, that through a long process of evolution, consciousness emerged and that eventually we all came into being. Everything that is will die, but Christians believe that love triumphs over death. Indeed, through love we create that which will endure for eternity.

It is not necessary to buy into every part of this story to get married in church. There are plenty of Christians, including some priests, who would want to take issue with some of the details. What exactly does it mean to talk of God as Trinity? In what sense can we survive death? Some Christians are agnostic, even sceptical, about parts of the story. Hence our insistence that the point of a church wedding service is that one is acknowledging that in the act of marriage one is discovering the real significance of life. Christianity in its understanding of marriage has gone a great deal further than this. It is not simply indicative of the reason for being, it is a great deal more than that. We turn now to look at some of the different accounts of marriage within the Christian tradition.

Support for delivery

A church wedding is a setting in which prayer is central. The first additional reason why a church wedding is considered important is because one is in an atmosphere of prayer. Prayer is the space that enables people to live and move within the life of God. The task in prayer is to take one's concerns and worries and locate them in the context of eternity.

As we know that the nature of eternity is loving and good, so we seek the support of love in confronting our worries.

At a wedding there is bound to be plenty of apprehension. It is of course an exceptionally happy time, but everyone who is married knows of the pressures and difficulties that all married couples are bound to encounter in their lives together. The adjustment to 'living together' can be tricky. The problems of managing the home's finances, dealing with decisions about jobs and careers, and handling the inevitable problems surrounding the rearing of children can create significant tensions. Christians believe that a community coming together to support a couple in prayer can make a difference.

Marriage realizes the purposes of creation

It was Jesus in St Mark's Gospel who explained that

marriage was grounded in the intentions of God right at the beginning of creation. It reads:

> He left that place and went to the region of Judea and beyond the Jordan. And crowds again gathered around him; and, as was his custom, he again taught them. Some Pharisees came, and to test him they asked, 'Is it lawful for a man to divorce his wife?' He answered them, 'What did Moses command you?' They said, 'Moses allowed a man to write a certificate of dismissal and to divorce her.' But Jesus said to them, 'Because of your hardness of heart he wrote this commandment for you. But from the beginning of creation, "God made them male and female." "For this reason a man shall leave his father and mother, and be joined to his wife, and the two shall become one flesh." So they are no longer two, but one flesh. Therefore what God has joined together, let no one separate.' (Mark 10.1–9)

In this account Jesus is going back to the Adam and Eve story in Genesis 2. Most Christians are quite happy to interpret the story of Adam and Eve as a poetic vision of the nature of all life. When Christians talk of creation, they are not simply referring to the origins of the universe, but also to the ongoing sustaining of the universe from moment to moment. The Adam and Eve story describes God's ongoing expectations for all human life. In Adam we can see a representative man, and in Eve we can see a representative woman. The text explains that Eve is to be a

31

helpmate for Adam. 'Then the LORD God said, "It is not good that the man should be alone; I will make him a helper as his partner"' (Genesis 2.18). Although some Christians might want to interpret this in a patriarchal and sexist way, it is clear that this is not what is intended. The relationship envisaged is one of equality. In the creation story, written much later than Genesis 2, but found earlier in the Bible in Genesis 1, the equality is made explicit:

> Then God said, 'Let us make humankind in our image, according to our likeness; and let them have dominion over the fish of the sea, and over the birds of the air, and over the cattle, and over all the wild animals of the earth, and over every creeping thing that creeps upon the earth.' So God created humankind in his image, in the image of God he created them; male and female he created them. (Genesis 1.26–27)

The point of the passage is that it is good and right that one man comes together with one woman forever. The stress of the passage is on mutual support (hence the helpmate or partner idea). This most basic of units, one person living with and loving another, is the means intended and blessed by God. We support each other in mutual commitment and love.

Marriage reflecting the covenant and the Church

In the Christian Old Testament (the Jewish Hebrew

Bible) we find the theme of marriage occurring in a number of different ways. The central way is that a marriage is an analogy of the relationship God has with his chosen people. Repeatedly, God represents the groom and Israel represents the bride. Sometimes the image is one of sadness: why does the bride ignore the love of the groom? Sometimes it is an image of commitment: as in marriage there is a promise of mutual commitment, so God is committed to his people.

In the New Testament, in his letter to the Church at Ephesus, St Paul turns marriage into an image that represents the relationship between Christ and the Church:

> Be subject to one another out of reverence for Christ. Wives, be subject to your husbands as you are to the Lord. For the husband is the head of the wife just as Christ is the head of the church, the body of which he is the Saviour. Just as the church is subject to Christ, so also wives ought to be, in everything, to their husbands. Husbands, love your wives, just as Christ loved the church and gave himself up for her, in order to make her holy by cleansing her with the washing of water and the word, so as to present the church to himself in splendour, without a spot or wrinkle or anything of the kind – yes, so that she may be holy and without blemish. In the same way, husbands should love their wives as they do their own bodies. He who loves his wife loves himself. (Ephesians 5.21–28)

St Paul's point is that a marriage is just like the relation-ship of Christ and the Church, and it should be one of complete love and mutual appreciation. However, it is worth noting that there are gender roles allocated: Christ represents the male and the Church represents the female. This is the source of the traditional expec-tation that women should obey their husbands (or in this translation be 'subject').

It is worth noting that although a wife is subject to a husband, a husband must love as much as Christ loved the Church, which was to the point of death. Nevertheless most Christians feel uncomfortable with such 'gender' imagery. The important point gleaned from this image is the one of mutual appreciation and deep commitment and love.

Marriage as a sacrament

In a large part of the Christian tradition marriage is viewed as a sacrament. This means that it represents a special vehicle of God's grace (i.e. God's bestowal of unmerited favour upon the institution and people of it). Although this view of marriage can be traced right back to the Early Church, it came to prominence in the late Middle Ages.

The best way to understand this account of marriage is to think of it in the following way. At the heart of each person is a 'soul'. It is the essence of your per-sonality and life. It is the life of you that survives beyond the grave. When you get married this 'soul' is combined with the soul of your partner and becomes one. In other words the sacrament of marriage involves God performing a miracle that brings your soul together with the soul of your partner. It is a fusion that creates an intrinsic unity. Once these two souls are brought together in the sacrament of marriage nothing can separate them. 'What God has joined together, let no man put asunder' (as the Church of England's Book of Common Prayer says).

This, as we saw earlier, is one of the reasons why divorce is impossible for the Roman Catholic tradition. God has joined two people together, therefore even if you want to separate that union, it is not possible. The Roman Catholic Catechism writes:

> Thus the marriage bond has been established by God himself in such a way that a marriage concluded and consummated between baptized persons can never be dissolved. The bond, which results from the free human act of the spouses and their consummation of the marriage, is a reality, henceforth irrevocable, and gives rise to a covenant guaranteed by God's fidelity. The Church does not have the power to contravene this disposition of divine wisdom. (Paragraph 1640)

The Roman Catholic Church does have the capacity to 'grant an annulment' (i.e. declare that no marriage ever took place). So if, for example, a person is not able to understand or make the promises made in a wedding ceremony, then it is possible that no marriage ever took place.

It is worth noting at this point that the Eastern

Orthodox Churches take a slightly differing view. They too believe that God takes the human contract and makes it an 'holy estate', but they also believe that marriages can break down. Using the notion of 'moral death', this tradition allows divorce and remarriage for many reasons.

Marriage as the setting for children

We deal with this as the last reason that Christians traditionally give for getting married, mainly because it is dealt with in the next chapter and because in the modern era it is not central. However, historically this has been a very important consideration. In the Church of England's Book of Common Prayer, written in 1662, this is the primary reason to get married. Marriage is linked with children and the family. Indeed, giving birth to children within marriage often looked like the primary goal. For some Christians, the procreation of children still has a central and all-important role within marriage.

Although in the modern era the churches still believe in the importance of marriage as the context for children, there is more emphasis on the intrinsic value of marriage for the married couple. In a world where contraception is easily available there are more choices for couples. Instead of children arriving during the initial years of marriage, couples often wait for five or ten years. These different lifestyle decisions make it important that marriage is justified for other reasons.

So why marry in church?

We finish this chapter where we started. A wedding ceremony marks the start of a marriage. All weddings, wherever they take place, are significant. They all mark a public witness to the love that two people have for each other. However, a church wedding makes certain themes clearer. The fact that the promises are made within a supportive community provides a setting in which the marriage can be supported and sustained. The church building witnesses to the significance of love as the very reason for being. The concept of covenant reflects the way that marriage mirrors the relationship between God and the world. The idea of the 'sacrament of marriage' reflects the miracle of what God is doing in human lives as two people make their promises together in the church. Finally, the church wedding provides the context for a marriage which is the home for the creation of a family. It is to this whole theme of parenting that we turn next.

CHAPTER FOUR

Parenthood

One of the major reasons why parenthood and marriage often go together is that the same unconditional love is involved in both kinds of relationships. We have already looked at this in some detail. When you opt to have children, you are opting for a relationship which will always be a part of your life. Henceforth you will always be a father or a mother, even if you do not wish to recognize that fact.

The relationship between parenthood and marriage is one that keeps changing. For centuries, there was an indissoluble link: marriage involved sex and sex always carried the possibility of children. The major risk and anxiety of having sex outside marriage was pregnancy and childbearing. With the options presented by the varieties of contraception and later the legalization of abortion, this changed. People could get married and opt not to have children. The link between marriage and parenthood became weaker. However, today with the growing respectability of cohabitation, we find the link returning. Many now opt to get married, when they decide they want children. Without children many of these couples might continue just to cohabit.

Thinking through the issue of children is essential.

Such are the connections, it is important that there is mutual understanding and also, preferably, agreement. The first issue is whether both parties in a couple agree that the marriage will involve children. The second issue is whether both agree on the basic parameters of raising children. It is to these two issues that we now turn.

Planning to have children

It is both a privilege and an awkwardness that families can be planned. It is a privilege because it means that the planning can take into account decisions about careers and finance. It is an awkwardness because nature still insists on having its say about the possibility of having children. There are many different eventualities that couples ought to think about prior to getting married.

Eventuality number one is that both partners are agreed that they would rather not have children. The childless state is currently rather fashionable. Often the most fortunate of couples can decide that the excitement of a career, coupled with the delights of having two adult holidays a year and a reluctance to add to the world's population problem means that they will make a positive lifestyle choice not to have children. This is an understandable attitude, especially for those in their twenties, as many listen to parents endlessly moaning about the chore of sleepless nights and the hidden expenses incurred by apparently simple activities like going to the cinema (with the need for babysitters, taxis and all).

Let us be clear that there is nothing at all wrong about this decision, although we had better warn you that those who choose such a path may well encounter plenty of disapproval, especially from would-be grandparents. Of course, a problem with this decision is that people can, and do, change their minds. It is difficult in your early twenties to know for sure how you will feel when the body clock is ticking and you are in your mid-thirties. This is a particular problem for women. As a woman enters her mid-thirties the risk of a pregnancy resulting in foetal abnormality, especially spina bifida, increases significantly. Although it is possible for a woman to have her first child in her forties, it is not necessarily very wise as it may bring further medical complications. For these reasons, the crisis about the issue of when to have children can be forced on the woman relatively early on in the marriage.

With eventuality number one must also go a commitment that each partner will be open to the feelings of the other. To make childlessness a condition for the marriage is harsh. It is one area where one cannot be too confident about how exactly one will feel in the future.

Eventuality number two is more widespread. It is the plan to have at least two children. If you feel that you are in this group, you have already been persuaded that the gifts and privileges of parenting far outweigh the drawbacks. It is one of the great privileges in life to watch a baby grow into a child, through teenage years and then into adulthood. It is exciting to provide support and construct an environment where virtue and love can thrive. Of course, such privileges will mean less sleep, more expense and hours of worry, but these pale into insignificance when set against the moments of amusement, awe and achievement that are guaranteed to run parallel with the drawbacks.

Very few parents actually regret having children, even if in a major row such a view is expressed. However, even this eventuality holds certain dangers that require some thought prior to getting married. The first danger is that there might be problems. The statistics are these: 80 per cent of couples manage to conceive naturally within two years. It is worth noting that successful conception can take up to at least two years. The moment a couple stops using contraception, their expectations are high. The plan is to have a child immediately. Some couples even expect pregnancy to occur that first month, say December, because they want a September baby who will be the oldest in its class at school. However, there are plenty of complexities that can thwart such detailed planning. The woman's ovulation only occurs for a few days, the fertilized ovum has a 60 per cent chance of not implanting in the wall of the uterus and there is a significant risk of natural expulsion of the foetus within the first three months. Even if things are all operating properly, one should not necessarily assume that it will not take some time.

Yet there is a possibility that conception, pregnancy and birth might not happen at all. Should this be the case, there are still other options available. Depending on the nature of the medical problem there are technologies that can assist the reproductive process. If, for example, the problem is the weakness of the male sperm, then artificial insemination of the strongest of the father's sperm will probably be able to correct the difficulty. If it is a more complicated problem the implantation of fertilized ova that have developed in a so-called test tube might succeed. But these processes are often expensive, not always successful and may carry ethical implications. Such issues ought at least to be discussed prior to getting married.

There is a third eventuality, especially pertinent to religious believers, which is simply to state that one hopes and trusts that one might be granted the blessing of children. This, of course, assumes that you are not one of the group which thinks that a childless life fits in better with the planned lifestyle. The advantage of this third possible eventuality is that it allows circumstance and opportunity to condition the ultimate plans in this area. The result is that one does not invest too much in any particular expectation. It is tragic when a marriage is sacrificed on the altar of unfulfilled parenting expectations.

Bringing up children

The issue of child-rearing is one that the vast majority of parents learn on the job. Plenty of people imagine that their children will be perfect and high ideals will be achieved. They may soon lose such principles as forbidding their children to eat sugary foods or crisps when later they find themselves sitting on a crowded train and they are struggling to keep a child quiet. However, there is a value in discussing the broad contours of policy. There are three areas that tend to be significant.

The first is the extent to which the faith dimension will prove significant in a child's life. Children can expose a significant fault line in the expectations of different parents. Right at the outset, almost straight after birth, there may be the problem of infant baptism (a 'christening'). On this question, different parents take different positions for different reasons. A parent who is agnostic might not wish to determine the child's choice of religion at birth, but would like to see it made by the free choice of the child as they get older. For a parent who perhaps is a member of a Baptist church, one should not get baptized until one has made a conscious decision as an adult to be a Christian. For others, it is important that the faith dimension in life is affirmed by the act of baptism. All these issues are discussed at greater length in our companion volume, *The Godparents' Handbook*.

As the child grows older so other issues may come to the fore. Parents will need to agree on domestic expectations made on the child. Plenty of parents discover the need to pray before meals and before going to bed when they have children. In a world where many go hungry, it is appropriate that one gives thanks for the fact of food on the table. At the end of a day, it is good to use the space afforded to remember others and reflect on the opportunities and difficulties of the day. Discussing these basic expectations as part

43

of one's marriage preparation can help in eliminating some of the problems that may arise later on.

The second area of policy is discipline and punishment. The tabloid newspapers love the debate surrounding smacking: is it appropriate to smack children or not? On the one hand, a sharp smack – especially when there is the possibility of danger to the child (e.g. when she is about to put her hand into the fire), or to others (she is about to sit on the baby) – may seem appropriate. On the other hand, parents are so much stronger than their children that to smack a child, even occasionally, can easily lead to smacks being given in rage or irritation. At points like these parents can significantly damage children both physically and psychologically. Many prefer to insist that methods other than smacking should be used. 'Time out' is probably the most effective. Here, when a child needs disciplining, one minute for each year of the child's age sitting in a corner or on a particular chair or on the stairs for misbehaviour can be quite effective.

The third area is schooling. The issues here are many and various. If one is in the fortunate position of being able to afford it, is it ever appropriate to send one's children to a private school? There are some who insist that the principle of the best education for all means that one should stay within the state sector and attempt to make it work as effectively as possible for one's child. Others feel that it is wrong to damage the child's prospects because of adult political principles. Education is an important topic, but one which can create significant tensions.

Naturally, parenting is an enormous area. There are many other issues and arguments that divide parents. Most will be worked out at the times they occur. However, taking a little time to think through some of the major issues of parenting prior to getting married will at least give you good practice in tackling the inevitable tricky topics when they arise.

Parents who are getting married

Some of those reading this book will already be parents. For all sorts of reasons there are large numbers of people who have children without getting married and, of course, there are others who have children from a previous marriage. The discussion outlined above still applies, the only difference being that it is likely there will already be actual opportunities and illustrations to discuss different models of parenthood.

However, existing children do pose additional issues. It is important when planning a wedding and there are already children from the current or previous relationships to make sure that the children are involved. Future marriage partners ought to be introduced to children in much the same way as, in time, you will expect to meet future boyfriends and girlfriends of these children. Views of parents and children should be expressed and handled with courtesy. This may be difficult if the view children have of your future partner is critical but it will be equally tricky when in time your views may be critical of their potential partners. All members of families have to learn to give partners about whom they might not feel particularly positive the benefit of the doubt. Ultimately children who have such feelings may well change their minds, but it is important that they feel able to express their views, especially if the views are critical. It is also important that children understand that it is not necessarily wrong to hold critical views about another person.

The problem in practice can be that the existing relationship between child and parent is so strong that the child is simply jealous of the new partner. This is very common and in most cases the problem disappears with time. Showing a tolerant and understanding disposition is important. The new partner must not resent a child discussing her own father or mother. It is wrong to expect all photograph albums in which the previous partner is prominent to be forgotten about or particular photographs removed. One ought to try and resist the temptation to criticize and attack the past. Allowing the past to be acknowledged and affirmed, in so far as one is able, is desirable.

Children and weddings

Existing children are now commonplace at weddings. It is important that if they wish they are given a prominent role on the day. A wedding is an occasion which needs many participants. There are vacancies for best man, bridesmaids, ushers, readers, speech-makers, musicians and entertainers. Often a father will turn to his oldest son to be his best man. Others use daughters to be bridesmaids. Whether in church or at the reception, it is often good if the couple can invite existing children to play a significant role in the proceedings. Giving them a role enables them to own the day and to share in the time of celebration.

Yet it may well be possible that children will find such a prospect all too difficult. This might extend to finding the whole concept of a parent getting married difficult. Naturally, children deciding that they really would rather not come to the wedding can be extremely upsetting, although it is a decision which can also be right. Much will depend on the circumstances in which the mother or father left: a painful divorce or bereavement can make it emotionally very difficult. Most children for their own mental stability try very hard to reach some sort of accommodation with the new situation. However, sad as it is for children that Mum is no longer around, they will still want to see Dad find happiness. The accommodation might involve attending the wedding but not taking part. If this is all the child can handle, then this should be welcomed and accepted.

The way forward in these tricky situations is to keep the channels of communication open and try very hard to understand the positions that others are taking. Weddings are, generally, happy occasions. But some will have feelings which are more ambiguous. It is difficult not to get annoyed with others, but it is important to try hard not to allow these annoyances to impair the relationship. Time will heal and this healing will reduce the complications. Showing understanding when the moment requires it will help speed up the process of healing.

We conclude this chapter with a few questions for couples to think about:

- Do we want children?
- In an ideal world when would that be?
- How would we cope if becoming pregnant proved difficult?
- What is our attitude to infertility treatments?
- Might we change our mind about any of these matters?
- What is the relationship between children and faith?
- Do we want to see our child baptized?

If we already have children prior to marriage, then the following questions are important:

- Have they been involved in the process of the relationship?
- Have we listened and understood their viewpoints?
- Are we keeping the lines of communication open?
- When it comes to planning the wedding, have we given some thought to a role our existing children can play?
- Are we ready to cope with their difficulties with the wedding?
- Are we determined to be constructive in our attitude to their difficulties?

CHAPTER FIVE

Practicalities and the Law

In this chapter we will unravel all the apparent complexities of the legal requirements of marriage and explain what precisely you will need to do to ensure that your marriage is legal. We will also give some practical advice on who you may need to contact for help in other matters (photographers, florists, etc.) and offer a checklist which will be of help to you in planning all the elements of your big day in plenty of time.

Legal requirements and restrictions

The laws of the various Churches in the UK generally reflect the laws of the land. This is because a wedding service is a legal ceremony and there are, therefore, certain requirements that must be met. Your priest will explain this to you and if you are unsure of this or any aspect of the arrangements – legal, religious or otherwise – please ask. Clergy have expert knowledge and years of experience of countless weddings: what you might think of as a problem can probably be ironed out very simply.

The law of England provides that every person (regardless of nationality) resident in a parish has a right to be married by banns in the parish church according to the rites and ceremonies of the Church of England (see 'Religious aspects: the Church of England' below). This is the case regardless of whether either or both of the couple are baptized but it is dependent on there being no legal impediment (see 'Who may marry' below). Indeed, because the Church of England is the Established Church of the land, any couple, one of whom is resident in the parish, may marry in the parish church, even if one or both of them are members of another religion. It is worth noting that the Vicar, Rector or Priest-in-charge of a parish church is not obliged to conduct a marriage themself, provided that they arrange for another Anglican clergyperson to take the service, but they must allow the parish church to be used.

Who may conduct a wedding ceremony

A legal marriage in England or Wales must be solemnized by an authorized person. This means a Registrar of any register office, an ordained minister of the Church of England or a minister of other religious denominations who have been legally authorized to register marriages. Scotland and Northern Ireland are mentioned in special sections below.

Who may marry

In the UK, weddings may take place only between a couple where one partner was born male and one partner was born female. Both partners must be over the age of 16. In England or Wales, if either is under 18 a parent or legal guardian must give written permission for the marriage to go ahead. If, however, someone under 18 has been married and is now divorced or widowed, this consent is not needed. Certain members of families may not marry. These couplings are set out in the Marriage Act of 1986. Many of these prohibited relationships will be obvious (you may not marry one of your siblings, for example) and others are rare, but similarly obvious (you may not marry, for example, the parent of a former wife or husband). Marriages between first cousins were previously prohibited, but they may now marry each other. Should you be in any doubt, clergy can provide you with a complete table of marriages that are prohibited by law.

When and where ceremonies may take place

Weddings may take place only between the hours of 8 a.m. and 6 p.m. Many years ago clandestine marriages used to take place under the cover of darkness. These timing restrictions were introduced to eradicate such unions. However, Quaker and Jewish ceremonies are exempt from these requirements, as are ceremonies conducted by special licence from either the Registrar General or the Archbishop of Canterbury. Such ceremonies are rare. Marriages where one or both of the couple are housebound or where one or both of the couple are detained as a prisoner or under the Mental

Health Act for at least three months may be solemnized by a Superintendent Registrar's Certificate at
the residence of the person who is housebound or
detained. Such weddings are less rare and may also take
place outside the hours between 8 a.m. and 6 p.m.
All marriages must be witnessed by two people over
the age of 18, both of whom must then sign the
marriage register.

Second marriages

No one who is already married to a living spouse may
marry someone else. If a person does go through a
second marriage ceremony in such circumstances, the
second marriage is invalid and the person is committing
the crime of bigamy. Widows or widowers may, of
course, remarry, in either a civil or religious ceremony.
There is no limit on the number of times a person
may marry, but they must be legally free to do so; that
is, their previous marriage must have been dissolved
and a decree absolute granted.

However, although the law of the land allows
divorcees to remarry, many clergy feel unable to
perform a second wedding. The Roman Catholic
Church forbids remarriage of divorcees. The Church
of England is moving to a position where, subject to a
careful analysis of the reasons for the breakdown for
the first marriage, divorcees may be permitted to get
remarried in church. Increasingly a number of clergy
ignore church rules and are happy to conduct wedding
ceremonies for those who have been divorced. Even

those who are not willing to conduct such weddings may well be willing to offer a service of blessing or dedication in church for a couple once a civil ceremony has taken place. More will be said about this service and how (in small ways) it differs from a wedding service in Chapter 7.

Marriage in Scotland

Although the days of young couples eloping to Gretna Green to be married at the blacksmith's forge with two passing strangers as witnesses are long gone, the law regarding marriage in Scotland is different from that in England and Wales (as it is in other legal matters too). Banns are not required to be read. Instead both members of the couple must complete a marriage notice form from a Registrar and inform the Registrar for the district in which the wedding is to take place. Fifteen days is the minimum legal period of notice required. In addition to the marriage notice, couples must produce birth certificates, a copy of any previous marriages' divorce decree or annulment (if applicable) and, if either of the couple lives outside the UK, a certificate that there is no legal impediment to marriage. If any of this paperwork is not written in English, a certified translation must be provided for the Registrar.

Marriage in Northern Ireland

Notice to marry here should be made to the District

Registrar of Marriages. The minimum legal period of residence prior to the wedding is seven days. As in Scotland, marriage cannot take place after banns, but by using a licence, a special licence, a certificate from a Registrar or a licence from a District Registrar of Marriage.

Marriage of foreign nationals

Although, as stated above, every person in England has the legal right to be married by banns in the local parish church, marriage by banns of foreigners is not always regarded as valid in some countries. In such case marriage in the parish church can still take place but using a licence.

Marrying abroad

Some people decide to get married in a country which is not their home, often combining this with having the honeymoon in some exotic location. Practical arrangements for this will be very different from those needed at home since almost certainly far fewer guests will attend the ceremony, but what few arrangements do need to be made will have to be organized from hundreds or thousands of miles away. The legal requirements will vary from country to country. Make sure that you know exactly what these requirements are well in advance of your wedding. Contact the embassy or consulate of the country where you intend to get married to obtain this information.

You will probably have to show your birth certificates (proving your age) together with proof of residence and, where necessary, a certificate showing that there is no impediment to marriage (proof of divorce).

Religious aspects

The Church of England

Marriage in the Church of England can be authorized in one of four ways:

- Publication of banns;
- Common licence;
- Special licence; and
- Superintendent Registrar's Certificate.

Banns are the easiest and most commonly used method. They involve notice of your forthcoming wedding being read out in both the bride's and the groom's parish churches on three consecutive Sundays during the three months before the wedding. When you visit the priest of the parish in which you live she will arrange for the banns to be 'called' (to use the technical term). If you both live in the same parish that is all that you need to do but if one of you lives in another parish then banns will have to be called there too. Visit the priest there also to arrange for this to be done. When this has been completed she will give you a piece of paper, called a banns certificate, to give the priest who will be marrying you.

When you make arrangements for the banns to be called in both the bride's and the groom's parishes you will need the same information. This is your full names, dates of birth, addresses from which you will be getting married, your occupations and your fathers' names. If you hope to get married in a church with a special attachment to you or your family (for instance, where you grew up or where your parents now live), you will need to use an address within that parish from which to get married. As well as this residential way of the banns being called, you may also have your banns called in a parish church where you regularly worship, but in whose parish you do not live. Either way, it is customary for couples to attend the calling of their banns. These will take place during the main act of worship on Sundays. Attendance will help you feel more comfortable with the church surroundings and this will have obvious benefits in terms of your nervousness on the big day.

Common licences are a quicker method than banns but more expensive. Only one full day's notice needs to be given before the licence is issued. As with banns there is a residential requirement but a common licence is a good safety net if there has been a slip-up with calling the banns. Your priest will be able to advise you on how to obtain one of these licences.

Special licences are issued only in exceptional circumstances or in emergencies and are costly to obtain. They are issued by the Faculty Office of the Archbishop of

Canterbury and allow a marriage according to the ceremony of the Church of England to take place at any time or place. In practice this usually means making it possible for a wedding to take place in a church which is not registered for marriages. Such places include college or university chapels.

Marriages by Superintendent Registrar's Certificate are also very rare. Residential requirements must be met and application must be made at least 21 days before the wedding. Such certificates allow couples to be married in a Church of England church without the resident priest's permission and for the ceremony to be conducted by someone who is not an ordained member of the Church of England (for instance, a friend who is a minister overseas or of another church).

Roman Catholic Church

Arrangements for getting married in a Roman Catholic Church are largely similar to those of the Church of England. The main difference, however, is that the marriage cannot be performed by banns but only by common licence or Superintendent Registrar's Certificate. Your priest will be able to advise on how all these preliminaries can be done. If one of the partners is a Roman Catholic and the wedding is to take place in a church which is not Catholic, some Catholic priests will require discussions with the couple to ensure that the Catholic partner will maintain their faith. In addition, it may be that promises as to how any children will be brought up will have to be made.

Orthodox Churches

Arrangements in Orthodox Churches are similar to those in the Roman Catholic Church.

Free Churches

Marriages that take place in Protestant churches other than the Church of England are solemnized using a common licence or Superintendent Registrar's Certificate. If the denomination is very small the ministers of the Church may not be authorized to register marriages. If this is the case the (civil) Registrar will need to be in attendance at the ceremony. She will not conduct the service but will record the marriage in her register.

The Society of Friends (Quakers)

For a wedding to take place in a Quaker meeting house, an application must be made to the registering officer at the Friends' monthly meeting. Following this, application notice of the marriage will have to be posted in the usual way at the local registry office. At the end of the period of notice (21 days) a Superintendent Registrar's Certificate will be issued which must be presented at the meeting house on the day of the wedding.

Wedding planner checklist

Organizing a wedding can be a fraught and stressful business. Alternatively, it can be an enjoyable and confident time. In order that the latter is the case for you, here is a countdown checklist of what needs to be done in the months before your wedding.

Twelve to six months

- Announce your forthcoming marriage to family and friends (you may also like to announce this in the newspapers).
- Select an engagement ring (if the future bride desires one).
- Write letters of thanks to family members or friends who give engagement presents.
- Decide on the venue, day and time for the wedding. Remember that churches often have more than one wedding on some days and it might not be possible to have the day and time you desire. Visit the priest and ask if it would be possible to have a certain day and time, rather than making immovable demands.
- Arrange to meet with both sets of parents to decide who will be financially responsible for which parts of the wedding budget. To help you to do this, get some estimates of costs (for the church, flowers, cars, clothes hire, reception, etc.).
- Decide who you want as best man, bridesmaids and ushers. Ask them if they are willing to perform

these tasks. You may like to ask others to take part in the service by leading the prayers or doing a reading. Decide too what all these people will wear on the wedding day.

- Decide the number of guests to be invited to the wedding (remember that it is often sensible to consult your parents in this).
- Book a venue for the reception and decide what sort of catering you would like (buffet, sit-down meal, etc.).
- Start to make a wedding present list.
- Book holiday time from work for your honeymoon.

Six months

- Book the cars that will be used to transport the bride and bridesmaids to the church and the couple from the church.
- Book any music that will be played at the reception (band, disco, etc).
- Book a photographer and a video firm if desired.
- Book a hotel for the wedding night.
- Buy or make arrangements to have made or hire dresses for the bride and bridesmaids.

Four months

- Visit the priest at the church where you will be getting married to arrange when the banns will be called. Discuss with her the music and order of service as well as the day and time for the wedding rehearsal. Discuss also whether you want bells, a choir or flowers at the church. If applicable, visit the priest of the other parish to arrange for the banns to be called there too.

- Visit the florist and discuss colours and types of flowers. This may include flowers for bride and bridesmaids, buttonholes for groom, best man, ushers and guests, as well as flowers for the church and reception.
- Send out wedding invitations, together with a finalized wedding list.

Three months

- Take out travel insurance for the honeymoon and consider general insurance for the wedding (reception disasters, etc.). Ensure that you both have passports that will be valid at the time of the honeymoon. Remember that airline tickets must be booked in the names that will be on your passports when you leave to go on honeymoon.
- Decide if you want service papers printed for the church. If so, order these, but remember to ask the priest to look at a copy before printing, to minimize any mistakes.
- Arrange to hire suits for the groom, best man, ushers and the fathers of the bride and groom.
- Shop for going-away outfits for bride and groom.
- Start to make a wedding cake or order it.

One month

- Buy wedding rings.
- Check arrangements with florists and car-hire firm.
- Check too the catering arrangements at the reception and advise on final number of guests.
- Meet the photographer and discuss the types of photos to be taken.
- Visit the doctor and arrange any injections that may be necessary for foreign travel.
- Obtain any foreign currency needed for the honeymoon.
- Buy any new clothes that will be needed for the honeymoon.
- Buy presents to give on the wedding day to best man, bridesmaids, ushers and any others taking part in the service. You may also like to give flowers to the mothers of the bride and groom at the reception – order these.
- Book hair appointments for bride and groom for a day shortly before the wedding (or even the day itself).

One week

Ensure that you have adequate amounts of cash to pay people who may need payment at the wedding (if requested, this might include fees for the priest, as well as payment for cars, florist or photographers).

CHAPTER SIX

Arrangements for the Big Day

In this chapter we will cover all the planning which you will need to do for the wedding day itself. To do this the chapter is divided into three main parts: 'Beforehand', 'Church' and 'Reception'. Where necessary we will give further explanation of the planning which was suggested in the last chapter. Although our planning lists and suggestions cannot be exhaustive (because every wedding is different and each couple will want to do things in their own way), what information is given should cover most eventualities that you might think of and some others besides. At the end of the chapter you will find a checklist which will help you on the wedding day itself. If you are able to look at this on the morning of your wedding day you will be able to put your mind at rest and reassure yourself that all arrangements are in place.

Beforehand

What to wear

One of the most basic things that you will need to decide when planning your wedding is what you and your guests will be wearing on the day. Obviously for the bride this decision may well be to wear a traditional white dress. For the groom, however, the choice is a little more varied. Certainly most grooms will want to wear a suit, but this is not the end of the matter. Perhaps the groom will want to wear a morning suit, in which case you will probably need to hire one. You might feel too that the best man, ushers and the couple's fathers could wear the same type of suit as the groom. If this is the case a fair amount of organization will be needed to make sure that all these people visit the suit hirers in plenty of time in order to be fitted before the day. Some grooms, especially if they come from a Scottish family, may choose to wear a kilt for the occasion. Others might feel that they want to wear something less conventional. Some grooms choose to wear a tie in the same colour as the bridesmaids' dresses, or to have all the key men taking part wearing similar ties, even if they are not wearing similar suits.

Flowers

Having chosen what you will be wearing you will need to decide what flowers, if any, you want on the day. The bride may want to carry a bouquet (a bunch of arranged flowers) and for her bridesmaids to carry flowers too. Here the colour of the dresses you have chosen may be crucial, as you will not want the colours of the dresses and those of the flowers to clash (one solution might be to have white flowers for everyone). Give some thought to the type of flowers you want as well as the colour. A good florist will be able to advise you on these matters. In addition to flowers for bride and bridesmaids, you will want to think about flowers, in the shape of buttonholes, for the groom, best man, parents of the bride and groom and pageboys. These can, of course, be of the same colour and type as for the women, but they need not be so. Additionally you may want to provide a buttonhole for all your guests (and it will be the best man's job to see that these get to the church safely and the ushers' job to distribute them). Whatever flowers you choose remember to tell the priest what these will be and she will be able to pass on this information to those who will be arranging the church flowers, if you are having them.

Transport

Transport for weddings can be tricky but need not be so. You will need to think about how the bride and her father and the groom and best man will get to church. Many couples will choose to hire two special, perhaps vintage, cars for the day. The first of these can be used to transport the bride and her father to church and later the newly married couple to the reception. The second car can be used to transport the bridesmaids. The groom, best man and ushers make their own way to the wedding, but remember that should the groom drive to church, the best man or someone else must be qualified and insured to drive this car to the reception as it may be needed as the 'going away' car. Car-hire companies are busy all year round so think about what transport you require and book it early. Some vintage-car enthusiasts hire out their vehicles for weddings and other occasions to help pay for their hobby. Whether you use a car-hire firm or a private individual it is a good idea to get written agreement as to what you require and what will be provided on the day.

Presents

Consider drawing up a list of the presents which you would like to receive as wedding gifts. Include a full range of differently priced gifts so no one feels that they have to buy you a boat or a holiday home in the south of France. Some large department stores will hold copies of your list for you. Instead of sending out a list to all those who are attending the wedding, simply tell your guests where the list is being held and the store will be able to advise your guests directly. Not only does this make things easier for you and for your guests but also it ensures that you do not end up with 15 toasters but no plates! As well as sending out your own wedding list, remember that you should buy 'thank you' presents for some of the key players on the day, which can be presented at the reception. You may consider small tokens of your appreciation for the best man, bridesmaids, ushers and pageboys. Some couples also like to present bouquets of flowers to the mother of the bride and of the groom. The best man should ensure that the presents, and any flowers, are taken to the reception.

Honeymoon

A traditional part of any wedding celebration is the honeymoon. Traditionally the groom used to plan the honeymoon and kept it a secret from his bride until after the wedding. Today, however, couples like to plan things more equally and decide where they want to spend this special time (this latter approach also saves the groom for the embarrassment of booking the honeymoon in some exotic location which the bride does not fancy visiting at all). Remember that if you have already been on holiday earlier in the year this may restrict the time you can have away from work for your honeymoon. Wherever you decide to go, and however long you decide to go for, more planning than simply booking the holiday with a travel agent will be needed. If the bride is to change her name on the wedding day she will need to arrange for her passport to be changed beforehand. She will need to obtain a form from the post office which will need to be signed by the priest who will officiate at the wedding. If she does not make this change then she can travel in her maiden name. The golden rule here is that the name on the passport and on the ticket must be the same. If your honeymoon is to be abroad, you will also need to obtain travellers cheques or foreign currency before you plan to travel, as well as any visas that may be necessary to enter a particular country. It is also wise to visit your doctor and have any immunizations against tropical diseases and to check that your tetanus and polio immunizations are also up to date.

Accommodation

Because your wedding day is likely to be long and tiring, you may choose to stay locally for the first night of your married life, rather than travel a long distance. A local hotel or the venue for your reception might be more convenient than having to book in two hours before a flight and then having a 10-hour flight halfway around the world. Some of your guests may also like to stay locally rather than have to face a drive home (or abstain from alcohol so that they can drive). It may be a good idea, therefore, to include a list of local hotels with your wedding invitation. If you want to avoid your guests over breakfast the next morning, either order breakfast in bed or make sure that you are staying in a hotel of which no one else has the details!

Insurance

Weddings are often a very costly business and so it may well be worth considering taking out some insurance to guard against things going wrong. Many insurance companies have plans designed especially for weddings, but if they do not you can always insure specific items (for instance, if you are having an open-air reception you might consider insuring against the famous British summer weather of heavy rain!).

Who pays?

Because marriage is a social institution the question of who pays for what at a wedding has immense variation. Many couples today pay for the wedding themselves and allow both sets of parents to make a contribution or pay for a specific item required at the wedding. It may be that the couple getting married are not so young, have savings of their own and may even be financially better off than their parents. Many parents, however, feel that it is their 'duty' to pay for a daughter's wedding. You can see then that resolving 'who pays for what?' is a potential minefield, requiring delicate handling. 'Traditionally' (whatever that means), the bride's father paid for: press announcements of the engagement and wedding; the bride's and bridesmaids' dresses; the photographer; wedding stationery (invitations, service papers, etc.); flowers for the church and reception; the reception. Traditionally also the groom paid for: the hire or buying of his own clothes; bouquets for the bride and bridesmaids; flowers for himself, best man, ushers, pageboys and the other guests; flowers for both mothers (to be given at the reception); costs of the church (fees, marriage certificate, organist, choir, bells); engagement and wedding rings; presents for the best man, ushers and bridesmaids; transport for himself and best man to the church and for himself and the bride to the reception (i.e. the car earlier used by her and her father to get to church); the honeymoon.

Church

Photographer

Although the planning of a wedding can take many, many hours of your time over a number of months strangely when the day arrives it may go by as in a flash, and your memories may not be as full as you might have imagined. One of the most common features of a wedding day mentioned by brides and grooms is that they scarcely had time to see, let alone talk to, many of the guests at the wedding. Because of this, a good set of photographs recording the occasion is high on the list of priorities of many wedding couples. To ensure that the occasion is well recorded it is important to find a good photographer. A recommendation of a professional photographer is a good starting point for this. Professional photographers will be able to show you examples of their previous work and give a quote of how much their services will cost. If their costs are too expensive because you are planning a wedding on a small budget, you might like to ask certain guests to send you sets of their snaps which they have taken on the day. Many couples ask friends to do this even if they also are using a professional photographer as such snaps will record moments of the day not usually captured by professional photographers. As with arranging many things concerning the wedding, you will need to book your photographer well in advance. Be clear when booking what poses and subjects will be taken. Photographers usually have a series of shots which they expect to take but are also only too happy to receive instructions for other ideas. Ensure that your photographer speaks to the priest before the wedding. Such a conversation will be to everyone's advantage as the photographer will get the shots wanted, and the priest will not have the service disrupted.

Video

Nearly all households in the UK now possess a video recorder and it is hardly surprising, therefore, that many couples choose not only to have still photography of their wedding day but a video recording as well. There are professional video-recording companies that special-ize in recording weddings and other events, but since wedding videos are not on show in the same way that wedding photographs are, some people choose to have friends to video the day for them. The advantages of the quality of pictures when using a professional rather than an amateur are obvious, however. Contact your video-recording company early as often summer dates are booked far in advance. Tell the priest that you intend to have a video made of your wedding, as there may be copyright fees to pay if music is recorded.

Music, readings and prayers

There is much to be decided upon and a huge variety of choices when it comes to thinking about the music you might want at your wedding. Choices will have to be made about processional and recessional music (i.e. music the bride walks in to and music the bride and groom walk out to), as well as what hymns and other choral music you want. Readings during the ceremony may obviously come from the Bible, but with negotiation with the priest it will probably be possible to include a reading from other sources too (a favourite piece of poetry, for example). Some of the prayers used in church marriage services are set and have to be used but there is plenty of scope for you to include other prayers too. In order to consider all these possibilities properly, the whole of Chapter 8 is devoted to looking at these choices.

Service sheets

Having decided on the details of the wedding service, many couples choose to have printed sheets giving the congregation the order and words which are to be used during the service. Details of how such sheets can be laid out will be given in the next chapter. Some couples may decide that they will produce service sheets themselves on home computers. Other couples may decide that they want a professional printer to do the job for them. This latter option may cost more but will mean that the service papers can be ordered with the wedding invitations and can be printed on the same type of paper. If you do decide to have service papers, of whatever type, it is important that you do not leave their production to the last minute. Typing up and printing service papers can be a pretty time-consuming process and you should neither give the printer a last-minute order nor try and produce them yourselves the night before.

Organist, choir and bells

If you intend to sing some hymns at your wedding you will need an organist to accompany the congregation. Nearly all churches have their own organist and when you see the priest to book the wedding she will probably ask you if you would like also to book the organist. There will be a charge for this, of course, but the sound of all your guests singing unaccompanied may not be one you would like to consider! If you would like a piece of music to be sung (an anthem) during the signing of the registers or at another point in the service, then ask the priest too about the possibility of a choir at the service. Not all churches have a choir nowadays, though many still do. If a choir is not available but you would really like to have an anthem, consider hiring a group of singers to come to the church for the occasion. Your priest may well have some contact names and numbers. In addition to organ and choral music, many church weddings are also beautified by the sound of bells. Not all churches have a peal of bells, but if yours does you may well want to ask the bellringers to ring for you. Many people feel that the sound of bells ringing as guests arrive at church together with the sound of them ringing again as the bride and groom exit the church at the end of the service and as the photographs are taken is a wonderful addition to the occasion.

Flowers

Most couples will want to plan the flowers used at their wedding around the type of wedding they are having and the clothes which are to be worn on the day. The bride's bouquet is not, of course, absolutely necessary but most brides decide that they would like to carry flowers of some sort. A good starting point in choosing flowers is to visit a decent florist who may well have pictures of different sorts of bouquet arrangements and will be able to offer advice on type and colours of flowers. Flowers that the bridesmaids might carry will need to complement their dresses, so it is perhaps best to choose the colours and style of the dresses before making decisions about the flowers. Both the bride and the bridesmaids may want to wear headdresses which are made from, or incorporate, some flowers. Buttonholes or corsages for the groom, best man, ushers, pageboys and other guests can be chosen at the same time as flowers for bride and bridesmaids. Here again it will be important to consider the style of suits to be worn by the groom and attendants and any colours which may in worn in ties, waistcoats or breast-pocket handkerchiefs.

Flowers at the church can almost certainly be chosen and booked by seeing the priest when organizing the rest of the service details. Many churches have a number of flower arrangers who provide experience and practical help in organizing the flowers. They will be able to provide you with the flowers and colours you require and, if there is more than one wedding on the same day, may be able organize sharing the costs of the flowers with the other couples. The kinds of flowers often arranged in churches at weddings are arrangements on the ends of the pews and pedestal arrangements, which might be in the porch, at the chancel step where the vows are exchanged and at the altar where the prayers and final blessing may take place.

Reception

Type of reception

The number of guests at your wedding will, in large part, determine the size of reception you have (the reception, with food, is also sometimes known as the wedding breakfast). If your guests number a hundred or so, you will need to arrange for the reception to be held in a hall or other large venue or perhaps for it to be held in a large marquee. If you are having fewer guests, however, then you might consider holding the reception at a hotel. Some couples choose to hold their reception at their own home or at one of the homes of their parents, perhaps with a marquee in the garden. If you choose this last option, it will undoubtedly involve more work for you all (even if you do not do the catering yourselves, the disruption will be enormous).

Besides deciding the venue for the reception you also need to choose the type of food that you will provide. You may opt for a formal, sit-down meal, with three, four or more courses or, alternatively, perhaps a buffet. Buffets can either be finger buffets, where there is no need for knives and forks and guests can move around the reception venue as they please, or fork buffets, where cutlery is needed and arrangements are slightly more formal with seating arrangements required. Whatever kind of food you decide on, ask your caterers for sample menus and full costings. Ask them too what their arrangements are for vegetarians or those with other special dietary requirements. You will need also to think about the drinks that will be provided. Champagne or cocktails are usually served as guests arrive from church at the reception and for the toasts. Various types of wine will be needed for the differing kinds of food that are served and so the food and the wine are best chosen hand in hand. Reception venues and caterers are often booked up to a year or more in advance. The reception, perhaps more than any other aspect of the wedding, therefore needs to be planned well in advance.

Table plan

If you choose to have a sit-down reception, whether as a formal meal or as a buffet, the caterers will need to receive from you a seating plan. It is a good idea to draw up this plan soon after you have received all the replies to your invitation. This might seem unduly hasty but seating arrangements can be complicated and it is as well to allow plenty of time for the planning to be done. Not only will you need to decide who sits where and with whom but also the caterers will need adequate time to write the cards which will be placed on the tables at the reception. It may be that a large table plan will also need to be drawn up so that guests can more easily see where they are to sit.

Before you begin to plan anything to do with the seating ask the caterers for a sketch of the table arrangements. This should give you an idea of how many people can sit at each table and how the tables can be arranged in the room. Having seen this plan, next organize the top table. This should consist of the bridal couple in the middle with their parents either side (it is customary for the bride's mother to sit next to the groom's father and for the groom's mother to sit next to the bride's father). Also on the top table should be the best man and chief bridesmaid (seated together) and, if room, other bridesmaids and the couple's brothers and sisters. The couple's wider family (siblings, grandparents, aunts and uncles, cousins, etc.) are usually seated at the tables nearest to the top table. Aside from these plans, you may seat the rest of the guests as you please. Some couples like to sit friends together while other couples like to arrange for people who have never had the chance to meet and talk before to have that opportunity. While any young children who are attending will need to sit with their parents, you might like to consider organizing a table specially designated for older children. A further point to remember when planning the seating arrangements is the potential problem of divorced parents. This is a situation that needs to be handled delicately. It may be that divorced parents are happy to be sociable together for your wedding day but, equally, some may not feel that this is possible. However you arrange things you will need to act with delicacy and tact. Partners of remarried parents will also need to be included in your planning.

Speeches

Normally three speeches are made at wedding receptions. The first speech is made by the bride's father. In his speech he thanks people for attending the service and reception, praises the groom and finally toasts the happy couple. The best speeches are those which are entertaining and hold the guests' attention. In this first speech then, as well as praising the groom, the father of the bride may make a joke at his daughter's expense (for example, 'I do not look on this event as losing a daughter, more gaining a bathroom').

The second speech is made by the groom. As he rises he thanks the previous speaker (his new father-in-law) and then goes on to make a number of other thank yous. He should thank the bridesmaids, pageboys, ushers and best man (perhaps including a funny story about him). He will thank the bride's parents for helping organize the wedding and hosting the reception (if they have). He should also thank everybody for attending and for their gifts. He should conclude by toasting the bridesmaids. Since this book is intended primarily for any future brides and grooms it may be useful for us to include fuller notes as to what the groom might say. A typical speech might:

1 Thank the bride's father for his kind words.
2 Say what a wonderful day today is turning out to be.
3 Say thanks to any family or friends who helped with flowers, cake, etc.
4 Include thanks to his parents.
5 Tell an amusing or touching story concerning his wife.
6 Say how beautiful she looks, today especially.
7 Show appreciation for the help of best man and bridesmaids.
8 Offer a toast to the bridesmaids.

The final speech is the best man's. He traditionally replies on behalf of the bridesmaids and thanks the groom for his appreciation. He should praise the bride and groom and also thank the host. The best man's speech usually includes a brief history of his friendship with the groom and may well include more than one joke at his expense. It is also the best man's task to read any telegrams or cards that have been received from people unable to attend the wedding. Although this is the usual order of speeches, it need not be so. Someone other than the bride's father might give the first speech, for instance, or the couple themselves may both like to speak rather than the groom alone.

Presents

It is usual at wedding receptions for the bride and groom to give small gifts to those who have been attendants during the day. The groom can thank those concerned and present the gifts publicly as part of his speech (especially useful if he has little to say!). Gifts ought to be given to the bridesmaids and can also be given to the best man and ushers. It might be that you also would like to give a token of your appreciation to any other people who have worked hard to make the day go well, even though they have not had a role on the day itself. Such people may include family members or friends who have made the wedding cake or the bride and bridesmaids' dresses, etc. Many couples also choose to present their mothers with bouquets of flowers.

Cake

One of the most photographed moments of a reception is the cutting of the cake. Some caterers who cook and serve the food at receptions also make the cake. However, more often than not, wedding cakes have to be organized separately from the rest of the reception meal. Traditional wedding cakes have a number of tiers and are made from fruitcake (it is said that the first cake of this type was made by a baker in Ludgate Hill, London, near to a church, designed by Sir Christopher Wren, with a tiered spire: St Bride's, Fleet Street). If this is the type of cake you choose it would be a good idea to order the cake some months in advance of the wedding as they have to be made, allowed to mature, marzipanned, iced and decorated. Other cakes may require less time, for instance, sponge or smaller, ready-made cakes. Some couples are lucky enough to have a friend or a relative who offers to make the cake for them. Whether you are in this position or choose to employ a professional cake-maker or baker, the cake will have to be safely transported to the reception. This is usually done with the separate tiers in their own boxes and the cake is then assembled at the reception venue. You will need to establish who will transport and assemble the cake for you. The person to do this might be a family member or friend, the baker or those running the reception venue.

During the reception it is traditional for the bride and groom to make the first cut of the cake before it is taken away to be sliced up before being served to the guests. The best man should announce to the guests when this is about to happen. An essential tip to remember when cutting the cake is to make the incision in the bottom tier of the cake – if you cut a higher tier the whole edifice may come tumbling down! You may be expected to hold this pose of making the first cut for some time while people take photographs of event.

Entertainment

The question of whether to provide entertainment during the evening of the reception is not a straight-forward one. Much will depend upon the time of the wedding service. If the service in church is in the morning, you may not want to have an evening entertainment after the wedding breakfast as this will almost certainly mean a very long day for all concerned. Conversely, a wedding is a supremely important occasion and you may wish to prolong the day as much as possible. Timing at the other end of the day may also be important. You may have a flight to catch mid-evening, for instance. Consider also the guests to your wedding. If most of them have a long journey to make home, evening entertainment may not be appropriate for them. These considerations aside, many couples like to enjoy a long and happy wedding day with as many people as possible. Evening entertainment does offer the chance to invite people who you have been unable to invite earlier in the day. Because of the size of the church or the size of the reception venue, or simply because of cost, most weddings have to be limited in the number of guests attending. An evening of entertainment, then, allows couples to share their day with even more friends and colleagues. Some caterers can organize music for the evening (a live band or a disco) although many do not offer this. It may still be possible for you to organize the music yourself with those running the reception offering the venue.

Alternatively, you might think of holding a separate, evening reception, away from the wedding breakfast. Food could be provided here too if you wished, though it would not be expected. As with most things that need organizing for a wedding, early booking of a band or a disco is advisable.

Going away

Unsurprisingly, like much of your wedding day, the ritual of 'going away' needs to be planned too. The departure of the bride and groom (which should be announced by the best man) can act as a signal to the guests that they may now leave if they wish. If you are going away directly from the reception's wedding breakfast, it is usual for the bride and groom to go to a room at the reception venue and change from their wedding clothes into less formal attire. If you are going away from the evening's entertainment, you may have already changed before the evening began. Either way, it is important that the transport for this has been organized. You may need to book a taxi to take you to your overnight accommodation or to the airport. Rather than use a taxi some couples arrange for a family member or friend to drive them away (perhaps both sets of parents will want to see the newly married couple off at the airport, for example).

Alternatively, you may be driving yourselves off on honeymoon. If this is the case, remember that the best man or some other designated person will have had to bring your car from home to the reception, as you will both have come in the car originally used to transport the bride and her father to church. If you do not use a taxi, it is important that the person who will be driving you remembers that this will be their task later in the day, as they will need to be sure that they do not drink too much champagne or other alcoholic drink at the reception.

Wedding day checklist

If you organize everything methodically and in plenty of time there should be no last-minute panics for your wedding. The following checklist tells you what final checking arrangements need to be done on the day itself. Although the list is not long, nor complicated, do not attempt to check these yourself. We recommend that the best man can look at this list and ensure that everything is in place.

- *Dress and suits* Do all the key players have the clothing which they require for the wedding?
- *Flowers* Are the bouquets and buttonholes with the key players for when they put on their wedding clothes? Are the buttonholes and corsages ready to be taken to the church if the florist is not doing this?
- *Service papers* Are the service papers ready to be taken to church?
- *Rings* Are the rings in the best man's suit pocket?
- *Money* Does the best man have payment ready for anyone who needs paying for their services on the day?
- *Speeches* Do the best man, father of the bride and groom have their speeches in their suit pockets?
- *Presents* Are the presents for the attendants and flowers for the mothers ready to be taken to the reception?
- *Transport* Have bookings been made for any taxis that will be required?

- *Clothes and passports* Do the couple have their going away clothes, together with suitcases for the honeymoon and their passports, ready to be taken to the reception? Do they have foreign currency?

CHAPTER SEVEN

The Wedding Service

In this chapter we will look at the arrangements, etiquette and wording of the marriage service. Having read this chapter, and having attended a rehearsal of the service at the church with the priest, you should feel more confident about your part, and the parts of others, in the wedding service.

Choosing a time

When you see the priest to book the date of your wedding you will also have to arrange a time for the service to take place. An element of this decision may be made for you. As there are approximately 150,000 church weddings each year in the United Kingdom, many churches will have more than one wedding on a given day. In some heavily populated areas, especially during the summer when weddings are more likely to take place, it is not unknown for there to be half a dozen or so services on a single day. Although such cases are rare you might be grateful just to get the day you want, let alone the time. Be prepared to be flexible on the time you want. Clergy want each wedding they take to go ahead smoothly, without any feeling of rushing. To enable this to happen, each service needs to be well spaced out from any other services taking place that day. Although the service will only take half an hour or so, the priest must allow time for guests to arrive, the service itself, photographs to be taken and for the couple and congregation to depart. Only then can guests for the next wedding begin to arrive if the church is going to avoid appearing to be a conveyor belt, churning out services.

As mentioned previously, weddings must take place between 8 a.m. and 6 p.m. Many couples choose a midday time for their service. This allows for the service, photographs and greeting guests at the reception in time for a late reception lunch around 2 o'clock. Other couples opt for a time much later in the day, after lunch but in time for an evening reception and meal. Choose your time in consultation with the priest and with an eye to the needs of caterers and those organizing the reception. Remember that if you are going to get married in the autumn or winter, then it can get dark by late afternoon and any pictures taken outside are likely to appear gloomy. A further factor to consider is the distance that many of your guests may have to travel to attend your wedding. If, for instance, many guests are unable to travel the night before the wedding owing to work or other factors and have to travel on the wedding day itself, they may not appreciate a 10 o'clock wedding! Remember that you want the day to be a happy and memorable experience for all those attending, not just for yourselves.

The rehearsal

It is usual, when you meet the priest a few months before the wedding to arrange the calling of the banns, for her to suggest a date and time for a wedding rehearsal. Often this will be in the week before the wedding. The reason for it being so close to the wedding itself is so that a long period of time does not elapse between rehearsal and service, allowing everyone taking part to forget what they are supposed to do. A good time for the rehearsal is the evening before the wedding. This may at first seem a little strange to you (why leave it to the last minute when there is so much else that might need to be done?). However, the evening before is an excellent time for a number of reasons. It allows everyone with a particular role to have the part that they have to play fresh in their minds and it also allows you to have a meeting with the priest to iron out any last-minute hitches that may have occurred. Most importantly, it makes the best practical sense. A wedding rehearsal the week before or even earlier in the week is not the most convenient time for people to attend. All the key players in the wedding are certain to be around the night before but may not be able to attend earlier than that (especially if you are getting married at a place some way from where you live).

The following people should attend the rehearsal: bride and groom; the best man; the person who will walk the bride down the aisle (most often her father); the bridesmaids; the ushers; any others taking a special part (those reading or playing a special piece of music for example). If a friend or family member is going to make a video of the wedding it is also a good idea for them to attend the rehearsal too in order to arrange with the priest where is the best place to stand without getting in the way or appearing too obtrusive.

Arriving on the wedding day

Arrival of the groom, best man and ushers

It is usual for the groom to arrive at the church before the bride. He does not need to be there to greet the guests (though many guests would feel this was a nice touch if he did) as some of the guests may arrive very early for the service, having travelled a long distance that day to attend. At least half an hour before the start of the service is the time we would recommend for arrival. This will allow the photographers time to take some photographs of the groom arriving, the groom with the best man and the groom with the ushers. The ushers will be arriving the earliest of all, in order to greet the guests, give them service papers or hymn books and show them to their seats.

About 15 minutes before the start of the service, the groom should take his seat at the front of the church, on the right-hand side nearest the aisle. The best man will sit next to him on his right. The rest of this row should be kept free so that the bridesmaids may sit down during the signing of the registers or during a choir anthem or other piece of music. The groom's close family will be immediately behind them and his friends and wider family behind them. Although people may come over to the groom to greet him and offer a word of encouragement, it is not a good idea for him to wander around the church saying hello to everyone.

Arrival of the bride's mother

A few minutes before the bride arrives it is usual for the bride's mother to be the last guest to take a seat. She may be accompanied to her place by a close male member of her family (a son or son-in-law, for instance). After she has taken her place no other guests should move about or take their seats, but instead should wait until the bride has made her entrance.

Arrival of the bride

About five minutes before the scheduled start of the service, the cars bringing the bride and her father and the bridesmaids arrive at the church. The chauffeurs of the cars will open the doors for the bridesmaids and for the bride's father. While the bridesmaids take themselves to the church door to meet the pageboys who will have already arrived earlier with their parents, the bride's father will open the door of the car for his daughter and then escort her to the church door. On this short walk to the church the photographer may well ask for some photographs to be posed for. At the entrance to the church, or in the church porch if there is one, further photographs may be taken and last-minute adjustments to clothing are made (the bride's veil for instance, or her father's tie). With such things to be done it can be seen that it is important that the bride's car does arrive five minutes before the start of the service and not later.

The order of service

Entrance of the bride

The priest will meet the bride and her father at the church door. When everyone is ready, a signal will be given to the organist to play the entrance music (this signal will be made by the priest, who will also ask the congregation to stand). For the procession the order will be: choir (if there is one), then the priest and then, 5 metres or so behind, the bride and her father. The bride should walk immediately on her father's right-hand side, taking his arm. Walking behind the bride will be the bridesmaids and pageboys. As this is happening the groom and best man should move forward from their pew to the right-hand side of the aisle (with the best man on the groom's right), facing the altar. The choir and priest will pass them as they stand in their places and, as the choir members take their places in the choir stalls, the priest will stop just after passing the groom and turn to face the bride as she walks up the aisle. When the bride is level with the groom she will stop and the ceremony begins.

When all are in their proper places and the entrance music has finished, the priest will welcome the congregation. Everyone remains standing for the first hymn, which is announced. While this is being sung the bride can lift her veil (with help from her father and a bridesmaid) and hand her bouquet to one of the bridesmaids. If the pageboys are very young it is a good idea for them to join their parents during the singing of the hymn, where they remain for the rest of the service. At the end of the hymn the wedding party (bride and her father, groom, best man and bridesmaids) remain standing, the congregation sit and the priest will continue with the service.

The introduction to the service which the priest now makes concerns what marriage is about, why people get married and what the responsibilities of marriage are. As the marriage is to take place in a church this will include an explanation of the theology of marriage and God's role in it. Each Christian denomination will have its own particular form of service, but all are broadly similar and any major differences are outlined at the end of this chapter. The priest's introduction underlines the seriousness of what is about to take place and stresses that the service will be taking place not only before the assembled families and friends but also before God.

Legal impediment

Next the priest will ask the congregation if they know of any legal reason why the couple may not marry. As was mentioned earlier in this book, the only reasons for the service to be halted at this point are: if either of the couple is already married; if they are related to each other in a way which prohibits marriage; if either of them is under the legal age of consent; or are aged 16 or 17 and do not have their parents' permission. The silence which hopefully follows the priest's question, often brings a few sniggers as people wait to see if someone will shout 'She is a trollop' or 'He is not good enough for my daughter.' Although this is almost certain not to happen, even if it did, these are not legal reasons to halt the marriage! Should a serious legal objection be raised the priest will take the couple, their parents and the objector into the vestry to investigate the claim. After addressing this question to the congregation, the priest will ask the couple themselves a similar question.

Declaration of intent

The priest will then ask each of the couple in turn (the groom first, then the bride) whether it is their intention to marry each other. This giving of their free consent is the first time in the service when either of the couple is required to speak. If there has been a hymn, the service has probably already taken five minutes or so, so there has been plenty of time for the couple to get over their nerves and to prepare to be centre stage for the rest of the service. The question is asked by the priest and the answer 'I will' should be addressed to her and not to the partner.

Giving away of the bride

In former times, when a woman was regarded as her father's property until she married and thus became the property of her husband, the small ceremony of 'giving away' the bride had some significance. A woman who married would bring to her marriage a dowry of money, property or possessions, as a gift from her father to her new husband. Today, of course, such a thing does not happen in the UK but the ancient ceremony remains. Traditionally the priest asked the question, 'Who gives this woman to be married to this man?' at which point the bride's father would take her right hand, give it to the priest, who then gave it to the groom. In some modern services, such an action is optional, or perhaps takes place without the accompanying question. This, of course, reflects changes in modern family life. Often the bride, and groom, have already left their family home and established a home life of their own. It is important to realize then that this part of the service is optional and has no specific legal or religious significance.

Exchange of the vows

Having given their consent, the couple now turn to face each other, as for the next part of the service they will be addressing each other rather than the priest or the congregation. Not only does this mean that they will be looking at one another for the most dramatic part of the service, but that the congregation will be able to see them better and feel more included in what is taking place.

First, the groom takes the bride's right hand in his and makes his vow to her. This can either be done by him having learnt the words by heart, by reading them from a service paper or, most usually, by him repeating them line by line after the priest. The priest will say the vows quietly and the groom will declaim them loud enough for the whole congregation to hear. When he has finished, the couple briefly break hands before the bride takes the groom's right hand in hers and makes her vows in the same way. An option is available here too: the bride may make an identical vow to the groom or if she wishes, additionally vow to 'obey'. As with the giving away of the bride, this reflects a different social attitude from today and so most brides choose not to 'obey'.

Giving of rings

With the vows having been made the couple now exchange a symbol of what has just been made. Although only one ring need be used (that which the groom gives to the bride), increasingly couples are exchanging rings with each giving and receiving a ring. Before this is done the priest will hold out a book for the best man to place the ring(s) on. Here again there may be a few sniggers as the congregation wait to see whether the best man has forgotten to bring the rings or if he drops them as he hands them over. The priest will then offer the book to the groom who picks up the bride's ring and places it on the third finger of her left hand. Because of nerves which cause people to sweat and their fingers to swell, it is almost certain that the ring will not fit over the knuckle of the finger easily. Do not panic at this point: the groom should simply place the ring over the finger as far as it will easily go and leave the bride to ease it into place when he has finished. As he holds the ring on the finger the groom says some words indicating what the ring stands for. If two rings are exchanged, the bride repeats the procedure with a second ring which the priest has also received from the best man.

The rings which are given in a marriage service serve as a physical reminder of the commitment which the couple have entered into. They also signify the love which the couple have for each other. The rings are made of a precious metal, just as their relationship is precious, and the rings also have no end, just as their love is to be everlasting. In medieval times it was believed that there was a vein which ran from the third finger of the left hand straight to the heart and thus the ring was placed on that particular finger.

Proclamation of marriage

The legal part of the service is now complete and so the priest addresses the congregation, proclaiming that the two individuals are now a married couple: husband and wife.

Blessing of the couple

In many services the couple are now asked to kneel in front of the priest. As a further symbol of what has taken place, she will join their right hands together, lift them up for all to see and may wrap her stole (the white scarf she wears around her neck as a sign of her ordination) around these joined hands and proclaim 'that which God has joined together, let no one divide'. These words are the words of Jesus and are taken from St Matthew's Gospel (Matthew 19.6). She will then pronounce God's blessing on the couple while making the sign of the cross over their heads. This blessing asks for God's protection and help in their new life together.

Signing of the registers

Because the couple are now married in the eyes of the law, the signing of the registers will probably take place at this point in the service (if it does not it will take place after the prayers). The signing of the registers may be arranged to be done either in the main body of the church so that the congregation can see all that happens or, if this does not prove to be practical, in a vestry or other room adjacent to the church. If the latter is the case then the bride and groom – together with their parents, best man, bridesmaids and witnesses – may disappear for a few minutes while the registers are signed. If the former is the case, most of the key players of the wedding may stay in their seats as only the bride, groom, priest and two witnesses have to sign the registers.

The witnesses may be any two people who have been present in the church to see the couple make their vows. Often they are friends of the couple, one each for the groom and the bride. They might also be members of the couple's families – perhaps one from each side. Three signatures are needed from each of these people: in two registers kept by the church and on a certificate which the couple take away with them. It is usual for the registers to be signed and then for the photographer to ask for a few pictures of the couple signing to be posed for. The registers will have been made up by the priest before the service but, even so, the process of signing the registers may take up to 10 minutes. Because of this, if there is a choir it may sing an anthem at this point, or if there is no choir the organist may play a piece of suitable music. The priest may then give the certificate to the groom or the best man to put in his pocket – here it is important that if he is wearing a hired suit he does not send it back to the hire company on Monday morning!

Holy Communion or Nuptial Mass

In some Christian traditions a wedding service may include a celebration of Holy Communion (also called the Mass). If this is so, the celebration will take place at this point, after the completion of the marriage. If such a celebration is not to take place (as is most likely), the service continues with the prayers.

Prayers

After the signing of the registers a reading may be given and/or a sermon may be preached. If not, a second hymn will be sung. During this hymn the newly married couple follow the priest to the altar rail from where, when the hymn is finished, the priest will lead the congregation in prayer. These prayers may include prayers for the couple and the families which each has joined, and perhaps prayers for the gift of children, though this is optional. The 'Our Father' will be used as a final prayer as this gives the congregation an opportunity to join in a prayer for the couple. After the prayers the congregation may stand to sing a final hymn.

Blessing and recession

A complicated manoeuvre now has to be completed by the couple before they exit church. After the final hymn the couple need to turn round to prepare to exit the church. However, they also need to change sides so that the groom is standing on the right and the bride is standing on the left as they lead the congregation out of church. This done, they walk arm-in-arm down the aisle while the organist plays a final piece of music. This is a special moment for the couple and they may walk as slowly as they like. They need to allow plenty of time for the official photographer, and others, to take the pictures that are wanted. As the couple lead the way they are followed by the best man and chief bridesmaid and other bridesmaids. It is then customary for the bride's mother to walk out with the groom's father and for the groom's mother to walk out with the bride's father. At the church door the photographer may ask the couple to pose for a few photographs. It is important that this does not last too long as the rest of the congregation may be trapped in the church and they will be anxious to get out into the churchyard and start taking photographs of their own.

Other denominations

Roman Catholic Church

As has been mentioned, Roman Catholic marriage services may also include a celebration of the Mass. Sometimes the couple are the only people to make their communion; at other times other members of the congregation may receive the sacrament. In the Roman Catholic Church, only baptized Catholics in good standing with the Church may make their communion. In Anglican, Methodist and United Reformed Churches, any Christians in good standing with their own Church may receive communion.

Another (minor) difference from the wedding service described above comes at the giving of the rings. It was traditional for the groom to place the ring on the thumb of the bride as he said 'in the name of the Father', on the index finger as he said 'in the name of the Son', on the middle finger as he said 'and of the Holy Ghost', and finally on the third finger as he said 'Amen'. Today, however, this is far from common.

Free Churches (Methodist, United Reformed, Baptist)

The marriage services in these denominations are very similar to the service in Anglican Churches described in the main part of this chapter.

Society of Friends (Quaker)

Quaker weddings are simple, quiet and solemn, very similar to the usual Society of Friends gathering on Sundays. Indeed, weddings take place as part of a gathering, with no leader but a group of people sharing in an act of worship. As they feel moved, the couple hold hands and say, 'Friends, I take my friend [name] to be my wife/husband, promising, through Divine assistance, to be unto her/him a loving and faithful husband/wife so long as we both on earth shall live.' Registers are signed by the couple and witnesses as in other Christian denominations, although often all those present also add their names. Rings may be exchanged after the promises have been made. As with any Quaker meeting, a wedding here will end with a period of silent communion during which time any attending may be inspired to express their thoughts or prayers. After about half an hour of silence the meeting may end with two of the elders of the meeting shaking hands.

Orthodox Churches

Weddings in Eastern Orthodox Churches (for instance, Greek or Russian Orthodox) may be substantially different from Western Christian church weddings. The service may not be in English but may be in Church Slavonic and may be much longer than the 30 minutes or so described in the services earlier in this chapter. Because it is highly unlikely that neither of the couple will come from an Orthodox family if they are to be married in an Orthodox church, any cultural differences can be explained by the family or, failing that, the priest who will be officiating at the service.

Service of blessing after a civil marriage

In Chapter 5, when we looked at the legal requirements surrounding marriage, we considered the relationship between the law of the land and the rules of the Churches. We saw that these two do not always go hand in hand and that there may be times when a church and its representatives, the clergy, feel unable to allow a marriage after divorce to take place. This problem is not unsolvable, however, and with a little effort you should be able to celebrate your marriage in church.

If your local priest is unwilling, through conscience,

to marry you in church, it may be possible for another priest to lead the service here. Perhaps you have a personal contact with a member of the clergy or perhaps a priest in a neighbouring parish may be willing to conduct the service for you in your own church with the local priest's permission. Some clergy are willing to marry people after divorce in their churches even if neither of the couple live in the parish. In such cases it may be that the priest will invite or require you to become a regular worshipper in her church for a time before the wedding.

Even if you are unable to find a priest to marry you after a divorce or are unable to find a church in which this might happen, there is still the excellent option of a service of blessing after civil marriage which is open to you. This service takes place in church after you have completed the legal formalities of being married in a registry office or another place licensed for marriages. The service in church can take place any time after the civil ceremony. In practice, however, many couples choose to have the two occasions as close together as possible. As many family and friends are likely to want to attend these occasions, many couples opt to have the wedding itself and the service on the same day. It may well be possible, for instance, to be married in the morning at the registry office and then to travel to the church for the service of blessing. If this does not prove to be practical, perhaps you could arrange the blessing to be on the day after the civil ceremony. Some couples may want to have a very quiet civil wedding followed by a much larger celebration with family and friends with a service in church. If this is the case, just the couple together with two witnesses need attend the civil ceremony and the emphasis can then be placed on what happens shortly afterwards in church.

It would take quite a well-trained eye to spot the small differences – of which there are a number – between a service of blessing and a marriage service. In essence the service is the same as the conventional church wedding described earlier in this chapter. We will, though, briefly look at what differences there are and explain why the changes are made.

Differences between marriage services and blessings

In essence a marriage service and a service of blessing are the same. Both services are occasions to celebrate the love between two persons, to make declarations of lifelong commitment and to ask for God's blessing on the relationship. Some differences in the form and content of service do occur, however. These are:

- *The entry of the bride.* Because a service of blessing takes place after a civil marriage ceremony, instead of the bride entering the church on the arm of her father, it may be that it is more appropriate for the married couple to enter the church together. As a newly married couple you might choose to enter the church in this way. Alternatively, having spoken to the priest, you might elect to have the bride enter in the conventional way and for the groom to be standing with his best man at the front of the church.

- *The introduction.* The opening to the service will be slightly different in wording from a marriage service. In addition to the introduction explaining what marriage is about, which is made at the beginning of a marriage service, the priest may add a sentence or two saying that you have come to church as husband and wife in order to dedicate your marriage to God and to ask for God's help in your married life together.

- *Legal impediment.* Because you will already be married there will be no legal impediment and so the question to the congregation and to the couple will be omitted.

- *Declaration of intent.* Again, because of your newly married status there will be no need to ask whether you intend to take each other as husband and wife. Instead, the priest will ask you both whether your understanding of marriage is that of the church. Your reply will be 'It is.'

- *Exchange of vows.* In turn you will both be asked whether you have resolved to be faithful to the other as long as you both shall live.

- *Blessing of ring(s).* This can either be done with the couple giving rings to each other in the conventional way or by the priest blessing the rings while they are already on the fingers of the couple.

- *Blessing of the couple.* This happens in the same way.

- *Signing of the registers.* This will not be done as you will already have a marriage certificate by this time.

- *Holy Communion or Nuptial Mass.* Identical to the wedding service if you so wish.
- *Prayers, readings and sermon.* These can all take place in the usual way and can be a useful way of involving others in the celebration. Perhaps older children from a previous marriage could lead the prayers or give the readings.
- *Blessing and recessional.* This can happen in the same way that it happens in the wedding service.

The other trappings associated with weddings such as best man, bridesmaids, ushers, choir, bells, flowers, etc. can all be had in a service of blessing. These are all important parts of the special day and the church is glad to help you celebrate your marriage by assisting in making it as memorable a day as is possible for the couple, their families and their friends.

CHAPTER EIGHT

Music, Readings and Prayers

With so much to organize in order to make your wedding day a success it can sometimes be easy to forget that what happens during the church service needs organizing too. We have already looked in the previous chapter at the order and content of the marriage ceremony. Most of this is, of course, prescribed in order to fulfil what the law requires for a wedding ceremony to be recognized as legal. In church services, however, there is also scope for the couple, in consultation with the priest, to have a significant input into the content of their wedding service. Through the choice of music, readings and prayers a couple can set the mood of the celebration and emphasize certain themes which appeal to them personally. For much of the wedding day the couple will have things said to them, in the form of speeches, telegrams and cards and other individual greetings. In selecting the music, readings and prayers which will be used as part of the church service a couple have the chance to share their thoughts about the day with their guests. In making these selections opportunities also arise to include a number of family members or friends in the service. People who are particularly close to the couple can be chosen to give one of the readings or to lead the prayers. Some couples are also lucky enough to have family or friends who are musically accomplished and who are delighted to be asked to use their talents during the wedding service. Organists, singers and other musicians can all be involved in such a way, if desired.

Music

There are a number of different types of music which can be played during a wedding service. Organ music can be played at the very beginning of the service during the entry of the bride and her father (processional music) and, at the end of the service, during the exit of the bride and groom (recessional music). There can be hymns and psalms sung by the whole congregation and there can be anthems sung by the choir during the signing of the registers or at some other point in the service.

Processional music

The most frequently played piece of organ music to accompany the bride as she is escorted up the aisle by her father at the beginning of the service is 'The Bridal March' from *Lohengrin* by Wagner. Many others are also often played and are listed below. A number of record companies now produce CDs with samples of music suitable for weddings and unless you have a firm idea of the music you want it may be a good idea to listen to one of these. Here are some suggestions that you may wish to listen to.

- Theme from 'St Anthony Chorale' by Brahms
- Prelude to a 'Te Deum' by Charpentier
- 'Prince of Denmark's March' by Clarke
- March on 'Lift up your Hearts' by Guilmant
- Hornpipe in D from the 'Water Music' by Handel
- Hornpipe in F from the 'Water Music' by Handel
- March from 'Scipio' by Handel
- Coro from the 'Water Music' by Handel
- Minuet No. 2 from the 'Water Music' by Handel
- 'Arrival of the Queen of Sheba' by Handel
- March from the 'Occasional Oratorio' by Handel
- 'Wedding Processional' by Harris
- 'A Trumpet Minuet' by Hollins
- 'Bridal March' by Parry
- 'Trumpet Tune' by Purcell
- Rondo from *Abdelazar* by Purcell
- Grand March from *Aïda* by Verdi
- Bridal March from *Richard III* by Walton
- 'Crown Imperial' by Walton

Hymns

There are a number of hymns which are specially written for wedding services and plenty of other general hymns which are well-suited for the occasion. Why not ask your priest if you can borrow a hymn book from church, in order to look at the words of various hymns, to help you in your choice. When choosing hymns it is worth remembering that some newer or less frequently sung hymns might not be known by your guests and that therefore the singing of these particular hymns at your wedding by the congregation might well be distinctly less than hearty! Listed below are the first lines of some of the most popular hymns chosen for weddings.

- 'Alleluia, sing to Jesus!'
- 'All creatures of our God and King'
- 'All people that on earth do dwell'
- 'All things bright and beautiful'
- 'Come down, O love divine'
- 'Dear Lord and Father of mankind'
- 'Father, hear the prayer we offer'
- 'Give me joy in my heart'
- 'Immortal, invisible, God only wise'
- 'Lead us, heavenly Father, lead us'
- 'Lord of all hopefulness'
- 'Love divine, all loves excelling'
- 'Morning has broken'
- 'Now thank we all our God'
- 'O Jesus, I have promised'
- 'O perfect love, all human thought transcending'
- 'O worship the King'
- 'Praise, my soul, the King of heaven'
- 'Praise to the Lord, the Almighty, the King of creation'
- 'The Lord's my shepherd'

Psalms

If your wedding is to include a celebration of Holy Communion or is to be a Nuptial Mass you will have the opportunity to choose a psalm to be sung. Usually a psalm (or sometimes another hymn) is sung immediately before the reading of the Gospel or between the first and second readings. It can be sung either by the whole congregation or by a choir. To help you make your choice look at a Bible (where the psalms are originally to be found) or a psalter (a book of psalms, set to music). The following are offered as suggestions for you to consider.

- Psalm 33
- Psalm 34
- Psalm 67
- Psalm 103
- Psalm 112
- Psalm 121
- Psalm 128
- Psalm 145
- Psalm 148

Music during the signing of the registers

The possibilities for music to be played during the signing of the registers are immense. If you are having a choir sing at your wedding, as well as singing for the hymns the choir will probably also sing an anthem during the signing of the registers (if you wish). The choir may well have an idea of the anthem it will sing but if you have a particular piece you could like to hear, suggest it to the priest. If there is no choir, perhaps you could have a small group of musicians play some instrumental music at this point. It might be that you have a number of friends who could play a piece of music together or one friend who could play solo. If not, it should be possible for you to hire a group of musicians either for the church service alone or also to play at the reception. Having some organ music played is also very popular while the registers are being signed. All church organists have some music suitable for such a time, although they are also delighted to play pieces that the couples suggest (providing the music is suitable for the organ). Unlike the processional and recessional music, at this point in the service, coming as it does so soon after the vows and exchange of rings, or after the prayers, organ music needs to be quiet and reflective. The following pieces are often thought by couples to be appropriate.

- Adagio in G minor by Albinoni
- Air from 'Suite in D' by Bach
- 'Sheep may safely graze' by Bach
- Adagio from 'Toccata, Adagio and Fugue' by Bach
- 'Jesu, Joy of Man's Desiring' by Bach
- 'Behold, a rose is blooming' by Brahms
- Minuet from *Berenice* by Handel
- Air from the 'Water Music' by Handel
- 'To a wild rose' by Macdowell

- Allegretto from Sonata No. 4 by Mendelssohn
- Romanze from 'Eine Kleine Nachtmusik' by Mozart
- 'Ave Maria' by Schubert
- 'Traumerei' by Schumann
- 'Chorale prelude on Rhosymedre' by Vaughan Williams
- Air from 'Three Pieces' by Wesley

Recessional music

It is usual for the bride and groom to leave the church while the organ is playing a piece of rousing and triumphant music. Some couples, however, choose to leave to a piece of choral music, sung by a choir, or to an instrumental piece played by a group of musicians (some brides choose to enter the church accompanied in this way too). If, like most, you choose to have a piece of organ music at the end of the service, you might like to consider the following, which are all popular.

- 'Grand Choeur in D' by Guilmant
- 'Festive Toccata' by Fletcher
- 'Now thank we all our God' by Karg-Elert
- Wedding March from *A Midsummer Night's Dream* by Mendelssohn
- 'Carrillon-Sortie' by Mulet
- 'Postlude in D' by Smart
- 'Carrillon in B flat' by Vierne
- Finale from Symphony No. 1 by Vierne

- 'Crown Imperial' by Walton
- 'Fanfare' by Whitlock
- Toccata from Symphony No. 5 by Widor

Readings

As we saw in Chapter 7, 'The Wedding Service', there
is scope for you to include readings from the Bible as
part of your marriage service. In the section below we
offer some suggestions which you might like to consider using. Each Bible reference is followed by a brief
description of what the passage is about. It is a good
idea to get a copy of a modern translation of the Bible
and read through the passages suggested. There may
be some passages which particularly appeal to you and
others which do not. This is fine; choose the reading
or readings which most reflect what you feel about
marriage and faith and want to tell others about in
the service. You also might like to look at more than
one translation of a passage as this might give a different
feel or emphasis to the reading. We suggest that you
begin by consulting the *New Revised Standard Version*
of the Bible.

Old Testament and Apocrypha

- *Genesis 1.26–28, 31.* The first story of creation
  where we are told that God created all things and
  that all things created by God are good. God com-
  mands women and men to care for the earth.
- *Genesis 2.18–24.* The second story of creation

where God the creator makes woman and man as partners for each other so that they can become 'one body'.

- *Genesis 24.48–51, 58–67.* Here acts of kindness by Rebecca show signs of God's love. Because of Rebecca's kindness (even towards a thirsty camel) she is chosen to be Isaac's wife.
- *Tobit 7.9–14.* The book of Tobit is not recognized by all Christians as being part of the Bible, but most agree with St Jerome that, together with some other named writings, it should be read for 'example of life and instruction of manners'. This passage talks of the unusual and enormous risk that accompanies the love of the woman Sarah and her future husband Tobias.
- *Tobit 8.4–9.* Tobias meets Sarah, a widow whose previous husbands have died on her wedding nights, and falls in love with her. On the eve of their wedding, Sarah and Tobias pray to God for a blessing on their marriage and for a long life together.
- *The Song of Songs 2.8–10, 14, 16; 8.6–7.* The Song of Songs is a poetry book which contains rich imagery of sexual love. In this passage young lovers describe their physical attraction to the other, their love and longing, and declare their faithfulness.
- *Sirah 26.1–4, 16–21.* Like Tobit, Sirah is one of the books of the Apocrypha, not fully recognized by all Christians. Sirah is a book of proverbs and these verses are proverbs of what it is to be a good wife, making it clear that wife and husband are dependent upon one another.

- *Jeremiah 31.31–34*. The prophet Jeremiah reminds the people of Israel that they are God's chosen people. He tells them that God will make a new covenant with them and that God's name will be 'written on their hearts'.

New Testament (Gospel readings)

- *Matthew 5.1–12.* These verses, called the Beatitudes, are part of the Sermon on the Mount where Jesus taught a large crowd of people. The Beatitudes are a guide to the kingdom of heaven, promising reward to those who endure the trial which life might throw at them now.
- *Matthew 5.13–16*. Also from the Sermon on the Mount, in this passage Jesus challenges his followers to be examples in this world, leading the life of the kingdom of heaven, enriching the lives of those around them.
- *Matthew 7.21, 24–29*. Here Jesus describes the wisdom of building a house on firm foundations and the folly of building a house on sand. So too is it with marriage; firm foundations are essential for a long and happy marriage. Those who practise what Jesus preached do not need to fear even a fierce storm.
- *Matthew 19.3–6 or Mark 10.6–9*. Jesus tells those who ask him about marriage that, as is written in Genesis, the marriage union between a man and a woman is divine and not just human. God created man and woman so that they might support each other.

- *Matthew 22.35–40.* In response to a question about which of the 613 commandments of the religious law was most important, Jesus says that the essence of them all is to love God and to love your neighbour as you love yourself.
- *John 2.1–11.* This story tells of Jesus's first miracle, turning water into wine, which he performed while attending a wedding. In telling the story, St John also wants us to understand that just as the water becoming wine is miraculous, so too is marriage. In marriage we have a foretaste of God's glory; lives are changed forever.
- *John 15.9–12.* Coming towards the end of St John's Gospel, this passage is of Jesus telling his disciples that he will soon be leaving them. His commandment to them is that they love one another, just as he loved them.
- *John 15.12–16.* Here Jesus calls his disciples 'friends' rather than slaves and says that friends are prepared to 'lay down their lives' for each other. The same can be true of marriage where partners 'die' to themselves each day for the sake of the other. In marriage, and in other relationships, when we lay down our lives for love we truly begin to live.
- *John 17.20–26.* Moments before he was arrested Jesus prayed for his followers, praying that they might be one just as he and the Father were one. Jesus recognized that only God could bring about this unity. In marriage, through love for one another, a couple can reveal God's love to the world.

New Testament (Epistles and other readings)

- *Romans 8.31–35, 37–39.* Writing to the Christians in Rome, St Paul tells the church there that nothing can come between humans and the love of Christ. Indeed, St Paul writes, through Christ salvation is available to all people. In marriage too, whatever problems come along, love can overcome them all.
- *Romans 12.1–2, 9–18.* Here St Paul writes that Christian love should be shown to everyone, not just other believers. Love, which is at the heart of the law, should include friends, strangers and enemies. In marriage, therefore, love should not just be for one's partner but for everyone.
- *1 Corinthians 6.13–15, 17–20.* A casual attitude towards sex is condemned in this passage. St Paul saw human bodies as 'temples of the Holy Spirit' and that therefore everything that we do with them should be holy. In what we do with our bodies, we can either honour or dishonour God.
- *1 Corinthians 12.31—13.8.* This is certainly the most frequently chosen reading at wedding services and it is not hard to see why. The reading speaks beautifully of what the qualities of love are and reminds us what we should and should not do. The passage says that no matter how many gifts or talents individuals might have, they are nothing if they do not have love.
- *Ephesians 5.2, 21–33 or, for a shorter version 5.2, 25–32.* The reading tells us that two people become one flesh in marriage. Such unions were willed by

God right from the beginning of time and are like the union between Christ and the Church. Some people, however, choose to ignore this passage for a wedding because they feel that it also tells of a social structure and attitude towards women that they cannot share. If so, the shorter version avoids this dilemma.

- *Colossians 3.12–17.* This is a very practical reading, telling those for whom it was intended how to live their lives. The author of the letter tells the readers that because they are chosen and loved by God they should live a life of love. It also tells them that whatever they do it needs to be done with God, as on their own they are bound to fall short.

- *1 John 3.18–24.* Written to a community which was divided, this reading tells the reader that unity and love are essentials for the Christian life. However, not only must the community love Christ, one another and be united; they must also put their love into action.

- *1 John 4.7–12.* An early heresy among the first Christians was the belief that having a special knowledge about God was all that was required to be saved (this belief was called 'gnosticism'). The author of this letter dismisses this idea and says that the proof of knowing God is loving other people. The passage says, 'God is love.' Later Christians thought of this when they wrote, 'Where charity and love are, God is there.'

- *Revelation 19.1, 5–9.* This passage belongs to a type of writing known as 'apocalyptic'. This style was concerned with the future and was intended to give hope to those suffering now. This reading may well be appropriate if you are regular churchgoers and your wedding is around Eastertime because it talks of the wedding between the Lamb (Christ) and the Bride (the Church). The reading tells us that this is a day of rejoicing at which all of heaven will sing 'Alleluia'.

Other readings

In conjunction with these biblical readings you might also like to consider choosing a reading from another source to be read aloud at your wedding. If you have a favourite poem or a piece of prose which you would like to use, or if you find another piece which you think might be suitable for the occasion, speak to the priest about this and show her the passage you have in mind. As well as a biblical reading (or perhaps instead of one) it should be possible for another, additional reading to be incorporated into the wedding ceremony. There are countless possible additional readings and to give you an idea of the range of literature available we include the following list which you might like to consider (some of which is poetry and some prose).

- 'He wishes for the cloths of heaven' by W. B. Yeats
- 'Love lies beyond the tomb' by John Clare
- 'Love's exchange' by Sir Philip Sidney
- 'Epithalamion' by Edmund Spenser
- Sonnet 18 by William Shakespeare

- Sonnet 116 by William Shakespeare
- 'Commitment' by Madeleine L'Engle
- *The Prophet* by Kahlil Gibran
- 'The beauty' by Thomas Hardy
- 'Marriage is one long conversation' by Robert Louis Stevenson
- 'The confirmation' by Edwin Muir
- 'The passionate shepherd to his love' by Christopher Marlowe
- 'For better, for worse' by Anatole France
- 'How do I love thee?' by Elizabeth Barrett Browning
- 'At the wedding service' by Gerard Manley Hopkins
- 'Thoughts on marriage' by Erasmus
- 'The good-morrow' by John Donne
- 'A birthday' by Christina Rossetti
- 'Never marry but for love' by William Penn
- 'Valentine' by John Fuller
- 'Song' by William Blake

Prayers

As we noted when we looked at the content of the wedding service earlier in this book, there is scope within the ceremony for the prayers to be led not only by a priest but by one of the guests also. For most weddings, the point in the service at which this can conveniently happen is for a family member or friend to lead the prayers which come before the final hymn. If your wedding includes Holy Communion or is a Nuptial Mass, then the prayers to be led will probably be called intercessions or the prayers of the faithful. Whichever of these two options applies to you, the basic format will be the same. In both cases prayers can be offered for the couple and for the families they are joining. The intentions of the prayers can also be widened to include other married people, those who are sick or who have died (especially deceased family members or friends), leaders of the church and world, and any others who need our prayers. If your wedding does not include Holy Communion or is not a Nuptial Mass, the prayers should conclude with the 'Our Father'. If they are concluded in such a way it is probably best if the traditional version of the prayer is used (which begins 'Our Father, who art in heaven, hallowed be thy name . . .'), rather than one of the more modern versions (beginning 'Our Father in heaven, hallowed be your name . . .'). More people are familiar with the traditional version, and those who do not know the more modern translations of the prayer may feel excluded by not being able to pray with others at this point. If, however, you decide to print a service paper (see the section at the end of this chapter) such problems need not arise. Your priest will be happy to provide you with some prayers for one of your guests to lead if you wish, or you might like to choose or write your own. The following selection of prayers is intended to give you an idea of the subject and style that you might consider using.

- *For the couple.* Creator God, maker of the universe, maker of woman and man in your own likeness, bless this couple (names) in their new life together. As they create their lives and their home together, may they turn to you in their sorrows, rejoice in you when they are glad and always be united in their love for you and each other, through Jesus Christ our Lord.

- *For those who are married*. Jesus Christ, Saviour and friend, we pray for all those who have been joined together in marriage. May their lives together witness to your love in our broken world, may unity overcome division, forgiveness heal injury and joy triumph over sorrow. This we ask for your own name's sake.

- *For the couple's relatives and friends*. Loving God, we thank you for the blessings we receive from you in our families and friends. With grateful hearts we remember the families of this couple. With (names) we thank you for the love and care which has guided them to maturity and prepared them for this day. In your loving kindness fill us all with a care and concern for others, that as we leave this place we may reflect your love for us among our family, friends and neighbours.

- *For those who are lonely*. O God of love, we pray for those who are lonely or who have no one they love who can pray for them. On such a day of happiness we remember too those who are unhappy. Whoever they are may they know your love, feel your blessing and be assured that they are not forgotten. This we ask in the name of Jesus Christ, the friend of all.

- *For the Church.* O God, make the doors of the Church wide enough to receive all who need human love and fellowship; narrow enough to shut out all envy, pride and strife. Make its threshold smooth enough to be no stumbling block to children, nor to straying feet, but rugged and strong enough to turn back the tempter's power. God, make the door of the Church the gateway to your eternal kingdom.

- *For the leaders of the world.* God of grace and gentleness, we pray for those who are called to lead our world and its communities. Give them wisdom and understanding, grant them courage and integrity and may their service to your people promote welfare and peace among all humanity. We ask this in the name of Jesus, Prince of Peace.

- *For those who are sick.* O loving Jesus, who stills the storm and soothes the fretful heart, look with compassion on those who are ill or anxious at this time; send the healing touch of your Holy Spirit to renew them in body, mind and spirit; may they be aware of your presence, supported by your power and comforted with your protection, now and always.

- *For those who have died.* Father of all, we pray for those whom we no longer see but continue to love. Especially we remember before you those family members and friends (names) who enriched the lives of many here today. In your loving kindness grant them the peace which you alone can give and fill them, and us, with the light of love, from this time forward and for evermore.

Service papers

Having chosen the music, readings and prayers for their marriage service, many couples decide that they would like to have service sheets printed which give the details concerning the order and words of the service. Although not absolutely necessary, service sheets do assist the congregation in following the order of the service, as well as making them feel more included in what is taking place. Service sheets can include the names of those taking part in the service (guests will, of course, know the names of the bride and groom but may not know those of the priest, readers or musicians). Many guests also like to keep the service paper as a memento of the day. Different types of service sheets give differing amounts of information. Some couples choose to have all of the words that are used in the service reproduced. The form of service sheet on page 127 is often used by couples and is given as an example of the minimum amount of information required on service sheets.

If you wish, you could add to this basic outline by including the full text of the words of introduction, the marriage vows, exchange of rings and prayers. If you are having a service of Holy Communion or a Nuptial Mass as part of your wedding celebration there will be substantial additions and changes to what is printed above. If this is the case you might like to produce a service booklet, with every word reproduced for the congregation, rather than a service sheet. This would certainly make the service easier to follow for those attending (though even in these circumstances it has been known for some people to look at the final pages of the service booklet first – as if they were looking at the sport pages of a newspaper, before reading the news!). Whatever form you decide to have for your service paper, your priest will be happy to give you a complete copy of the service if you ask for it. Alternatively, you can buy copies of the service from good bookshops, either printed separately or contained in a larger service book. It is a good idea to ask your priest to look over a draft of the service paper before you have final copies produced, as it would be a shame to have any mistakes or errors printed.

The Procession: *The Bridal March* (Wagner)

Introduction

Hymn: *Come down, O love Divine*
(the words of the hymn to be printed here)

The Marriage between
Imogen Mary Kearns
and
James David Paul Drury

Hymn: *Now thank we all our God*
(the words to be printed here)

The Signing of the Registers
during which *Prelude and Fugue in C* (Bach)
will be played

The Prayers

Hymn: *Praise, my soul, the King of heaven*
(the words to be printed here)

The Recession: *Wedding March* (Mendelssohn)

CHAPTER NINE

After the Honeymoon

This book is called *The Church Wedding Handbook* and not 'The Church Marriage Handbook'. Although the difference in the title might seem very small, it does show that the book is about the business of getting married and not about how marriages can be strengthened or improved. So although this is not a book written by two agony uncles to solve marital problems, we cannot finish at the honeymoon stage and simply wish you 'Good luck' but must say something about the things you will need to do on your return from this special holiday (perhaps via cloud nine!). You will have put a lot of effort into organizing the wedding day but the work does not end there. In this chapter we will look at the practical things which need to be done and some other things which ought to be done to make the whole wedding experience complete, and in the last chapter we touch on how to make the 'Christian' side of your wedding a framework that can support your marriage.

Tying up loose ends

The first set of practical things which need to be done on returning from honeymoon relates to tying up any loose ends concerning the arrangements for the wedding day. Some of these things may have been done by yourself or others immediately after the wedding (although it is as well to check that they have been done) and some things can be done only on your return. Incidentally, you may be interested to know the origin of the word 'honeymoon'. The word was first recorded as being in use in the middle of the sixteenth century and it was commonly assumed that the first month of marriage was regarded as being the 'sweetest time'.

Hired clothes

Any clothes which have been hired for the occasion should be returned to the shop as soon as they are no longer needed. Many shops charge a fee per day for the hire of suits, etc. and so it is in your own interest to return them promptly.

Be sure not to make the mistake of sending back a suit which has the marriage certificate in one of its pockets (many grooms or best men have been known to do this).

Press reports

Many couples, especially those who have announced their engagement or forthcoming wedding in the papers, choose to have a small report in the press about the wedding itself. This is usually paid for (unless one of you is a celebrity) and accompanied by a photograph.

Most local papers, and national ones too, have a staff member responsible for co-ordinating this section of the paper.

Expenses and bills

You must ensure that all those people whose services you employed on the day are paid in full swiftly. Many will have asked for payment in advance but others expect payment after the event. Remember that many who helped you on your wedding day are professional people who make their living by the service they offer. It is not fair to expect these people to live on thin air until you get round to paying your bill! You should also ask the best man if there are any out-of-pocket expenses which he incurred in relation to the wedding and see that he is reimbursed.

Thank yous

There are a number of people who you will need to thank for their part in making your wedding day so enjoyable and successful. Your parents will appreciate a brief note from you both as a newly wedded couple. Parents give much support in planning the wedding and therefore a letter saying thank you and sending your love is an opportunity to say something which is so often taken for granted and not so frequently expressed. Perhaps you could include a small present or bouquet of flowers too. You will also want to thank those who gave you wedding presents. Not only will you want to thank individuals, couples or families who gave presents, but remember to thank any work colleagues who may have taken a collection at work in order to give you a present collectively. Your brides-maids, best man, ushers and any other attendants will deserve a special thank you. When thanking these people you may want to include a photograph of you both taken on your wedding day (perhaps you could include also a photograph of the bridesmaids to the bridesmaids, a photograph of the best man to the best man, etc.). Others who may need thanking for their efforts in preparation for your wedding or for their efforts on the day include: caterers, cake-makers, dress-makers, photographers (both stills and video), flower arrangers, car drivers and any others who helped you in any way.

Distribute cake

It is traditional that those people who were invited to the wedding and were unable to attend are sent a piece of the wedding cake. It may be that you can use this opportunity to tell these people how the wedding day went and perhaps include a photograph or two. Alternatively, the task of distributing the cake might be one which you could ask your parents to undertake while you are away on honeymoon.

Photographs

If you have chosen to use a professional photographer,

the proofs of the wedding photographs should arrive soon after you arrive home from honeymoon, if not before. These will need to be gone through carefully and the photographs you want reproduced, and the quantities you require, selected. It is a good idea to ask your parents and the best man and bridesmaids whether they require any special shots for their own collection. If they do, it may be that you can give them these photographs as part of your 'thank you' to them.

Paperwork

There are a number of pieces of paperwork which may need to be attended to as you begin your married life together. While none of the items listed below need urgent attention, they will need some consideration at some point.

Name change

The majority of new brides decide to change their surname on marriage. Although this is customary, there are no legal or financial reasons why this must be so. Indeed, increasingly a number of brides are deciding either to keep their own, maiden name or to combine this with the surname of their husband to form a double-barrelled name. Some women choose to change their names in the social sphere but retain their maiden names for professional purposes. If the bride does decide to change her name there are a host of people and organizations who will need to be informed of the change. As well as needing a change of passport (which was discussed earlier in this book), in no particular order, the following may need to be notified: relatives; friends; employer; Inland Revenue; doctor; dentist; Department of Health; banks and building societies; electricity, gas and telephone companies; credit card companies; insurance companies; DVLA; any clubs and associations; mail-order catalogues; local authority (for voting purposes) and, if necessary, the Department of Social Security.

Making a will

Marriage automatically renders any previous wills invalid and, therefore, if you made a will before you were married you may need to make a new one after marriage. Many couples do not bother to make wills until they have children as the law states that on death the estate of a person goes to her or his next of kin (that is, in the case of a married person, the spouse). Although there are certain limits prescribed on how much can be automatically transferred in the absence of a will, for most married people without a will the issues of probate are straightforward. There are some circumstances, however, which complicate the issue (for example, children from another relationship) and therefore it is recommended that the advice of a solicitor be sought.

If before marriage either of you has already taken out a life assurance policy, you will probably want to make your spouse the beneficiary of the policy. If you have not taken out a policy you may both want to consider this, especially if you have a mortgage which is dependent upon you both being in work and able to make the repayments. Couples who also have children will need to pay special attention to the benefits of life assurance and the demerits of not having such a provision in place. If on marriage you move into a new home together, you may need to consider house insurance, both for the house itself and its contents (including all those new wedding presents). If, on the other hand, one of you moves into the established home of the other you may need to look at the insurance policy to ensure that any additional items are adequately covered.

Starting a family

Many couples find soon after their wedding that it is not long before people start to ask, 'When do we expect to hear the patter of tiny feet?' As we made clear earlier in this book, marriage is not about legitimizing the birth of children but is primarily about the commitment which two people want to make to each other. We discussed the different attitudes to parenting earlier. However, it is worth stressing at this point that such comments about when children are expected might annoy you or might delight you, but either way it is important that you have discussed the possibility of children as a couple and know how to reply when such questions are asked. Forms of contraception which have become available within the last generation now allow couples to choose when to have children in a way unimaginable to our forebears. Many people are choosing to have children much later in life than did previous generations. While such trends allow the younger generation to develop careers and independent living, older generations may find such choices baffling. It is important that any decisions you make as a couple are fully discussed and thought through and that these choices made are made known to others, when they ask, in a sensitive way.

Anniversaries

An anniversary is a yearly celebration of a special event. For married couples, wedding anniversaries are a chance to remember their wedding day and the family and friends who celebrated the day with them. Some anniversaries will be celebrated quietly at home on your own and others may be celebrated more publicly, with a dinner shared with others or perhaps with a party. Traditionally the anniversaries of 25, 50 and 60 years are marked by special celebrations. Many couples decide to mark each year of marriage with the giving of gifts and sometimes, especially after long periods of time, with a renewal of marriage vows made in public in church. Although some might view anniversaries as a chance for card companies to cash in on the human events, others see an anniversary as a chance to reflect on the time which has gone before and the time which is to come. The list below details wedding anniversaries and the items or materials which are associated with each. You may like to give a gift to each other on these anniversaries made out of the appropriate material or related to it.

1 Cotton	10 Tin	35 Coral
2 Paper	11 Steel	40 Ruby
3 Leather	12 Linen	45 Sapphire
4 Silk	13 Lace	50 Gold
5 Wood	14 Ivory	55 Emerald
6 Sugar	15 Crystal	60 Diamond
7 Wool	20 China	75 Second Diamond
8 Bronze	25 Silver	
9 Pottery	30 Pearl	

Prayers, poetry and prose

Just as the readings, music and prayers which you chose for your wedding service expressed what you felt about your marriage, there will be times during your married life when other pieces of music, readings and prayers will be able to give expression to some of your feelings at various points of your lives together. For many of us there are times in our human journeys when we do not feel able to find the words to describe the feelings we have or the emotions we feel.

It is at these times when the words of others can often fill the gaps we feel. Frustration at our own inadequacy can be dispelled by the reflections of similar experiences shared by others. As your married relationship grows, words written by others can often be of help, comfort, encouragement and strength. The following are classic examples of what some of the world's best-loved writers have written concerning their own relationships and the feelings surrounding them.

Future

Grant us, we beseech thee, O Lord, grace to follow thee whithersoever thou goest. In little daily duties to which thou callest us, bow down our wills to simple obedience, patience under pain or provocation, strict truthfulness of word or manner, humility and kindness. In great acts of duty or perfection, if thou shouldst call us to them, uplift us to sacrifice and heroic courage; that in all things, both small and great, we may be imitators of thy dear Son, even Jesus Christ our Lord.

Christina Rossetti

One flesh

While it is alive
Until Death touches it
While it and I lap one Air
Dwell in one Blood
Under one Sacrament
Show me Division can split or pare –

137

Love is like Life – merely longer
Love is like Death, during the Grave
Love is the Fellow of the Resurrection
Scooping up the Dust and chanting 'Live!'

Emily Dickinson

Togetherness

I ask but one thing of you, only one,
That always you will be my dream of you;
That never shall I wake to find untrue
All this I have believed and rested on,
Forever vanished, like a vision gone
Out into the night. Alas, how few
There are who strike in us a chord we knew
Existed, but so seldom heard its tone
We tremble at the half-forgotten sound.
The world is full of rude awakenings
And heaven-born castles shattered to the ground,
Yet still our human longing vainly clings
To a belief in beauty through all wrongs.
O stay your hand, and leave my heart its song!

Amy Lowell

Faithfulness

How do I love thee? Let me count the ways.
I love thee to the depth and breadth and height
My soul can reach, when feeling out of sight
For the ends of Being and ideal Grace.

I love thee to the level of every day's
Most quiet need, by sun and candlelight.
I love thee freely, as men strive for Right;
I love thee purely, as they turn from Praise;
I love thee with the passion put to use
In my old griefs, and with my childhood's faith.
I love thee with a love I seemed to lose
With my lost saints – I love thee with the breath,
Smiles, tears of all my life! – and, if God choose,
I shall but love thee better after death.

Elizabeth Barrett Browning

Forgiveness

Give them grace, when they hurt each other, to recognize and acknowledge their fault, and to seek each other's forgiveness and yours.

The Book of Common Prayer

Children

Through their devout love and unwearying care, the home, though it suffer the want and hardship of this valley of tears, may become for the children in its own way a foretaste of that paradise of delight in which the Creator placed the first members of the human race.

Pope Pius XI

Ageing

Grow old along with me!
The best is yet to be,
The last of life, for which the first was made:
Our times are in His hand
Who saith, 'A whole I planned,
Youth shows but half; trust God: see all,
    nor be afraid!'

Robert Browning

CHAPTER TEN

The Christian Spirit and Married Life

After the combination of hassle and excitement of the wedding and the honeymoon (all made easier by our helpful checklists), you return to your home to start married life. The whole idea of all that 'fuss' and all those presents is that the day should become a foundation for a life of mutual commitment. In this chapter we shall reflect a little on the ways that that can become a reality.

Love makes the difference

We have suggested that the main reason why you get married in church is because you want to witness to the nature of love. You have stood in a building dedicated to the Transcendent and declared your love one for the other as an expression of that transcendence. In other words, marriage is not simply an evolutionary device to encourage procreation but is the discovery of what really matters. This idea (this 'theology') is what the entire wedding service is all about.

For Christians, this discovery of love should never be taken for granted but should instead be a matter of eternal gratitude. Gratitude is likely to encourage respect and vigilance and it is important that the mutual commitment you feel expresses itself in constant reminders of the love you share.

Right at the outset of your married life adopt a strict rule: that you will always be grateful for the discovery you have both made and will ensure that the love between you both grows and develops. This will require the occasional check-up (to use a motoring image) or audit (to use an accountancy image). By check-up one means a conversation where one expresses everything one appreciates and everything one finds irritating. Appreciation is important because love depends on mutual affirmation. If one is constantly trampled underfoot, then the love rapidly turns into fear or resentment, but if one is affirmed, then the love grows in self-confidence. Explaining the irritants in life is important because irritations can, if neglected, become crises or significant differences.

Talking about the things that irritate might, on the face of it, sound rather unwise and you might imagine it would be more sensible to just keep quiet about such things. However, this sharing of problems is probably the greatest single difference before and after marriage. Before the marriage, one just wants to find similarities and build bridges. The fact that your partner has a passion for motorbikes that you find both stupid and boring is something hidden. Once inside a marriage what appeared a minor difference you could tolerate can become a significant difference, especially if it involves money. You should allow these issues to be discussed. With hobbies, or passions about such things as motorbikes, it is likely that you will have to learn to understand, respect and perhaps appreciate them, but you can probably agree to strict limits, especially in terms of finance and time.

Keeping love alive therefore often starts with conversation, including, occasionally, conversations about that which matters most: the love at the heart of your marriage.

Church and prayer

Marriage, at times, will be a challenge. However, it is a challenge that can often be best handled in the context of prayer and a supportive community. Marriage was never simply meant to be about two people sitting at home watching television every evening (as good as a soap opera about Liverpool might be!). Marriage provides you with support to interact in the Christian community, which in turn can support your marriage.

Some priests and pastors find that a couple who perhaps were not interested in church before they were married discover an interest in it after they get married. This is especially true if the priest has been supportive of the couple before and during the wedding. Finding a church can be good way of keeping the Christian spirit at the heart of your marriage alive. The Church, first and foremost, is a community consisting of a group of people who share a commitment to Christ and who want to express that commitment in regular meeting and participation in the sacraments.

The two main sacraments are baptism and the Eucharist (sometimes called Holy Communion or the Mass). The Eucharist involves reflecting on the story of love as it is embodied in the life, death and resurrection of Jesus. The eucharistic community (that is, those people who meet at church to share in the breaking of bread and drinking of the cup of wine) can be a reliable source of friends. Those in marriage, like all people, need good friends.

Naturally you can find churches which are unhappy communities. Sometimes a local church can lose sight of what matters and can become intolerant and intrusive. In such cases, instead of looking positively and constructively on those who are not part of the Christian community, the church is constantly erecting barriers and sending out intolerant signals. The problem is that there are passages in the Bible that seem to commend such an attitude to the outsider. Historically, these passages have been responsible for exceptional cruelty, for example, the Church has an appalling record on anti-Jewishness. However, most Christian communities are much more tolerant and positive and regard the God of the whole world as still interacting with those outside the Church: otherwise God would not be God. The authors of this book believe it is wrong to imagine that God is interested in only a small minority of humanity and is ignoring the rest or leaving them to the rule of Satan. If you start finding intolerant or sectarian attitudes in the church that you are attending, just leave and find another community. An intolerant church can create real difficulties: for individual members; for those outside the church; and for those inside who are married.

Once you have found a supportive community, it is good to get involved. We live in an age when involvement in many things can be tricky. The combination and lure of out-of-town shopping centres and satellite television is making it difficult to get people 'involved'. We prefer to 'shop till we drop' or enjoy an evening watching 'the telly'. From the Freemasons to political parties, all voluntary associations are struggling. We do not mind meeting up with a group of friends and going to the cinema or the pub, but supporting and sustaining an organization is regarded as too demanding by many. It is worth remembering, however, that when people moan about the decline in church attendance, this decline is actually less than the decline in almost all other forms of social organizations, from trade unions to the townswomen's guilds.

Yet there is a real danger here. These organizations provide a setting for people to grow or develop. Television can be largely passive, but real stimulation requires an organization and structure to deliver it. If you have been sufficiently persuaded by the argument from love to God, and then from God to getting married in church, perhaps you should find a little time to help the Church continue to thrive.

Linked with participation in a church is the personal discipline of prayer and worship. Many couples find it helpful both individually and as a couple to find time to pray together, perhaps spending 10 minutes in prayer together at the beginning or the end of the day.

For many people this can be embarrassing, especially on the first occasion. You might want to start by sharing silence together for five minutes and then perhaps introducing some prayers later. This sort of space is important because it becomes a way of offering up to God the problems and difficulties of the day.

Within many marriages, one person has a different attitude towards faith from that of the other. This is not surprising given that religion is but one factor among many that provide the context in which love develops. For various complex reasons, it is often the man who is less enthusiastic about religion. This can be tricky. The groom might agree, perhaps reluctantly, to a church wedding because it matters to the bride, but then regards the disruption every Sunday morning of going to church as 'unreasonable behaviour'. For many couples this is resolved by the wife making the journey to church and the husband staying tucked up in bed.

It can be useful to establish a few rules here. First, each partner should respect the integrity of the other. It is important to recognize that the faith journey is different for different people. People travel in many different directions. There are Christians who are a particular type of Christian when they marry but then change or move on as their life progresses. There are non-Christians who marry each other and then find faith together. There are also non-Christians who marry Christians and have to find some sort of understanding. This variation in arrangements is not something to fear but to accept. Acceptance requires recognition that it is not appropriate to constantly try and 'convert' the other. The atheist should not constantly mock faith and the Christian should not constantly leave religious tracts around the house. Rather, each should encourage the other in the practice of faith, whether this faith is implicit or explicit. Keeping faith alive is hard work and requires perseverance; one has to keep going. The act of love in a marriage encourages the partner who has religious faith to keep working at it.

Enjoy it all

Finally, a simple rule in marriage is to enjoy as much of it as is appropriate. You will go to bed every night with someone you love. You will give and receive more physical intimacy than most of your single friends. Most important of all, you will have a friend to discuss things with and to relate to. In short, you should have real enjoyment. It is important to value the moments when things are going well but it is important also to work through the problems. In doing so, the problems, when overcome, can become part of the pleasure of a happy marriage. We conclude then by wishing you long life, health, happiness and good luck.

Useful Addresses

As we have said a number of times in this book, most of the questions which you might have regarding the legal requirements and practicalities of your wedding ceremony will easily be dealt with by your local clergy. If you are unclear about any of the issues mentioned in this book, or indeed anything else, do not hesitate to contact them, as they will be only too pleased to help. However, if you need further advice you may find this contact list useful. It lists all the major Churches in Britain and Ireland, together with addresses for the Registrars' Offices in each region.

Baptist Union

Baptist House, 129 Broadway, Didcot, Oxfordshire, OX11 8RT

Catholic Marriage Advisory Council

Clitherow House, 1 Blythe Mews, Blythe Road, London, W14 0NW

Church of England

Enquiry Centre, General Synod of the Church of England, Church House, Dean's Yard, Great Smith Street, London, SW1P 3NZ

Church of Ireland

Church of Ireland House, Upper Rathmines, Dublin 6, Eire

Church in Wales

39 Cathedral Road, Cardiff, South Glamorgan, CF1 9XF

Church of Scotland

Department of Communication, 121 George Street, Edinburgh, EH2 4YN

Faculty Office of the Archbishop of Canterbury

1 The Sanctuary, London, SW1P 3JT

Registrar General for England and Wales

General Register Office, Smedley Hydro, Trafalgar Road, Berkdale, Southport, PR8 2HH

Registrar General for Guernsey

The Greffe, Royal Court House, St Peter Port, Guernsey, GY1 2PB

General Register Office for the Isle of Man

Finch Road, Douglas, Isle of Man

Superintendent Registrar for Jersey

States Offices, Royal Square, St Helier, Jersey, JE1 1DD

General Register Office for Scotland

New Register House, 3 West Register Street, Edinburgh, EH1 3YT

General Register Office for Northern Ireland

Oxford House, 49–55 Chichester Street, Belfast, BT1 4HL

General Register Office for the Republic of Ireland

Joyce House, 8–11 Lombard Street East, Dublin 2, Eire

Greek Orthodox Church

5 Craven Hill, London, W2 3EN

Lutheran Council

Lutheran Church House, 8 Collingham Gardens, London, SW5

Methodist Church Press Office

Westminster Central Hall, Storey's Gate, London, SW1H 9NH

Presbyterian Church in Ireland

Church House, Fisherwick Place, Belfast, BT1 6DW

Religious Society of Friends (Quakers)

Friends' House, 173–177 Euston Road, London, NW1 2BJ

Russian Orthodox Church

Cathedral of the Assumption and All Saints, Ennismore Gardens, London, SW7 1NH

Scottish Episcopal Church

21 Grosvenor Crescent, Edinburgh, EH12 5EE

Unitarian Church

Essex Hall, 1–6 Essex Street, London, WC2R 3HY

United Reformed Church

86 Tavistock Place, London, WC1H 9RT